MANOVE
149 Fuller St
Brookline
02146

Prices and Choices

Prices and Choices:

Microeconomic Vignettes

David Hemenway
Harvard University

Ballinger Publishing Company • Cambridge, Massachusetts
A Subsidiary of J.B. Lippincott Company

Copyright © 1977 by Ballinger Publishing Company. All rights reserved. No part
of this publication may be reproduced, stored in a retrieval system, or transmitted
in any form or by any means, electronic mechanical photocopy, recording or
otherwise, without the prior written consent of the publisher.

International Standard Book Number: 0-88410-663-2 (C)
0-88410-660-8 (P)

Library of Congress Catalog Card Number: 77-2733

Printed in the United States of America

Library of Congress Cataloging in Publication Data

Hemenway, David.
  Prices and choices.

  Includes bibliographical references.
  1. Microeconomics—Addresses, essays, lectures.
I. Title.
HB171.5.H394   330   77-2733
ISBN 0-88410-663-2
ISBN 0-88410-660-8 pbk.

Contents

Preface

This book is a collection of eighteen short, readable essays on some generally neglected topics in economics. It is aimed primarily at students past the introductory level. While it has no ideological axe to grind, it does illuminate some of the limitations as well as the applications of economic theory. But it is primarily a book that puts economic concepts to work, using tools of analysis that are well within the grasp of undergraduates. The essays are relevant and intrinsically interesting. Almost all of the topics covered are ones about which students have some general experience and ideas. Questions are included at the end of each article to supply fuel for discussion and thought.

Every college teaches intermediate price theory. Unfortunately, the microeconomic textbooks are often dry and formalistic. As a result, this second-level course has serious problems keeping students interested and happy. There do not seem to be any books containing essays specifically designed to provide supplementary readings and applications at this level. Where there are readers, these are usually collections of dry journal articles. *Prices and Choices* could fill a need in this area. Additionally, there are a wide variety of college courses in "economic analysis," "economic policy," and "applied economics" where the book could prove useful. And ther are now many economics courses given at professional graduate schools of design, public policy, law and health care that could profitably make the book required reading.

While *Prices and Choices* is intended primarily for students majoring in economics, it can be read with some benefit by laymen and economics professors. The articles cover a wide range of intriguing topics, and while some economic jargon is used, advanced economic analysis is not. The essays are intended to provide some interesting insights, and to require some thought and reflection by the reader. They are designed to be read, and an attempt has been made to keep them succinct, snappy, and entertaining.

Many friends read, commented on, and helped me with one or more of these essays, including economists Tom Schelling, David Harrison, and Ed Lazere, health policy students Suzanne Cashman and Dan Strouse, and retail magnates Linda I. Nordness, Sung-ja Moon Yuan, and Nancy Lou Hemenway. My deepest gratitude goes to Richard Caves for his continuing advice, assistance, and support.

My colleague, good buddy, and tennis partner Frederick Wales Gramlich carefully scrutinized the first draft of each article, and also coauthored the essay on haggling. I hope he caught the worst mistakes.

David Hemenway

Part I

Basic Assumptions

INTRODUCTION

A fundamental tenet of economic theory is that the purpose of all economic activity should be to satisfy the wants of consumers. Thus, production is not valued for its own sake, but solely as a means of increasing consumer utility. The economist has a tendency to identify consumption with final consumers, viewing employees, like machines, as inputs or resources. Therefore, the defense of any business solely on the grounds that it "creates jobs" is given little weight by economists, who view this primarily as a using up of scarce resources. The potential social and psychological benefits to workers from having a job, and their "on-the-job" consumption or utility from work time, are not *directly* taken into account.

Strong philosophic questions can be raised concerning the goal of satisfying consumer desires. Is a society that caters to every consumer whim really an ideal society? Should consumers be given everything they want? (We know, or believe, that children should not.) Are people's preferences always "good"? Aren't some desires more virtuous or of higher moral quality than others? Might not even Robinson Crusoe be somehow better off if not all his needs and desires were met? However you answer such questions, it is important to recognize the strong and controversial normative implications of this most basic of economic assumptions.

A closely related and fundamental postulate in economics is that man is a rational being. This simplifying assumption often differentiates the economic approach from that of the sociologist or psychologist. For example, when other social scientists explain criminality, they often employ such concepts as depravity, insanity, deprivation, deviance, and abnormality. These ideas are foreign to the economist. The economist depicts man as highly rational. A man may become a criminal, but only after carefully considering the other available options. He may select a career as a bank robber, but only because he perceives it as his best alternative; he may find that it pays well, the hours are good, and he is his own boss. The policy conclusions are obvious: the way to decrease the number of bank robbers is to make that occupation less attractive and others more so. Economists are beginning to use the rational-action assumption to explain virtually every human choice: why people walk on the grass, or pollute the environment, or brush their teeth, or even go to church.

The normative conclusions of microeconomics depend on the assumptions of excellent knowledge and high rationality: the individual needs to know all his alternatives and their outcomes; he must be able to order these alternatives in terms of his preferences; and he must then choose the most preferable. It is generally assumed that all this is done without cost. These are, of course, very strong assumptions.

There are complications, because many consumption decisions are made not by individuals, but by groups (for instance, the family). Economists generally disregard this problem. But even for an isolated individual, we may question whether behavior is normally highly rational. It is difficult to make transitive ordering of thousands of alternatives. (If you prefer A to B, and B to Z, you must prefer A to Z.) It is impossible to know all the ramifications of even the most important options. And people often find it hard not only to know what is best for themselves, but also to act in the way they would like. A "weak" individual is defined as one who often is unable to do what he thinks is best. If you hear someone saying "I drink too much," or "I wish I didn't goof off so much, or watch so much TV," or "Why can't I control my temper?" you are probably not listening to an "economic man." Think of people you know well. Are they usually highly rational? Are you? It is interesting to consider literary figures whom all of us can know intimately. How closely do they resemble economic man? Does a Madame Bovary seem highly rational? Or an Ahab? A Billy Budd, a Raskolnikov, a Heathcliff, or a Scrooge?

If the assumptions of excellent information and high rationality are broken, the normative conclusions of price theory do not follow, and many economic policy prescriptions become suspect. For example, if consumers do not choose rationally (or if one does not believe their wants should be satisfied), then the demand curve does not represent marginal social utility, or any such notion, and it is not clear that the restriction of supply by monopolists is necessarily bad.

Another related, vital assumption in microeconomics is that tastes are exogenous to the economic system. One might say that economists have taken John Donne's famous line and contorted it into "No! Man *is* an Island." But, of course, tastes, utility functions, and consumption decisions are interdependent among individuals; social forces do matter in our lives. The economic well-being of others can affect us directly, bringing joy or sorrow, envy or compassion. The actions of others affect our options and our happiness. Economic consumption is often most enjoyable when done jointly. Moreover, we continually compare our lives and station with others', and our perceived status can affect our contentment. This is clearly recognized in the economists' "demonstration effect" and "rising expectations" hypotheses that relate relative standing to preferences, utility, and consumption expenditures.

The social and economic environment certainly has some effect on an individual's tastes and preferences; yet to the extent tastes are endogenous to the system, the normative conclusions of price theory do not follow. It would surely be questionable to applaud an economic system that largely satisfies wants that it itself helped mold or create. Economist S. Alexander makes the point:

> That wants are generated by the social process, not in the trivial sense that they are affected by advertising, but in the profound sense of their dependence on the whole cultural matrix, certainly threatens the entire ethical basis of economics, striking in particular at Pareto-optimality. It challenges the principle that more is better, and opens up the question of what sort of wants we should generate, what sort of men we should make.[1]

Fundamental philosophic issues of this sort are generally excluded from consideration or discussion by the strong assumptions of the microeconomic model.

The four chapters in this section deal with issues related to the basic assumptions of micro theory. Emotional behavior is clearly important in the real world, but is usually ignored by economists. The first chapter discusses temptation, and tries to bring it within the purview of rational behavior. It argues that a wise individual will recognize the possibility of short-run temptation, of irrational behavior, and will attempt to structure his options and payoffs so as to minimize the expected harm. The analysis applies not only to temptation but to any emotion, such as fear, anger, infatuation, joy, or sorrow.

The economist's assumption of costless rationality means that an individual should find additional favorable possibilities or opportunities desirable. Chapter 2 describes some situations where this is not the case, where more options may prove detrimental. A purpose of this chapter on options is to discuss some of the actual problems of making decisions, and living with them.

Microeconomic theory normally excludes from consideration not only irrational behavior, but also endogenous changes in tastes. The theory does not examine why preferences change, since it takes them as exogenous, or given. Micro theory is thus of little use in explaining fashion, the continual and massive swings in taste that seem to occur in music, architecture, books, games, pets, etc. The third chapter focuses on changing styles in clothing. Relying heavily on the work of a few economists, it emphasizes the importance of consumption externalities in explaining fashion change in the clothing industry. The desire of individuals to conform, and the desire to demonstrate and achieve social distinction combine to create the constantly evolving dress styles that influence not only our expenditure for apparel, but also our aesthetic perceptions.

The final chapter emphasizes the crucial influence social forces and pressures have over individual action. It presents two fictional tales to illustrate the potential importance of such externalities and the possible inefficient and undesirable consequences that can result from decentralized decision making. The article also mentions how a simple postulate—that people desire status—can prove somewhat useful in explaining such phenomena as worker alienation and the neglect of public, relative to private, goods.

Economists clearly recognize the existence of consumption externalities, but often find them "so various and so difficult empirically to uncover that we usually assume simply that they do not exist."[2] The article on social forces argues that such an attitude is unfortunate and dangerous. It is unfortunate because it excludes from analysis much that is interesting and important; it is dangerous because the neglect of large externalities can lead to very incorrect and improper normative conclusions and policy prescriptions.

In sum, the chapters in this section are designed to focus the reader's attention on some of the fundamental, though often neglected, assumptions of microeconomic theory, and to help him gain a little better perspective on the relationship between the model and the real world. The chapters in the remaining parts of the book apply the general economic approach to a wide variety of issues and phenomena. This first section is therefore not intended to denigrate this useful way of thinking, but to highlight some of its implicit postulates, and to alert the reader to the fact that some of the normative or value conclusions of economics need to be taken with a grain of salt.

NOTES TO INTRODUCTION

1. Sidney Alexander, "Human Values and Economists' Values," in Sidney Hook (ed.) *Human Values and Economic Policy* (New York: N.Y.U. Press, 1967), p. 110.
2. Roger Sherman, *The Economics of Industry* (Boston: Little, Brown, 1974), p. 307.

OTHER SOURCES

Sidney Hook (ed.), *Human Values and Economic Policy.*
Sherman Roy Krupp (ed.), *The Structure of Economic Science* (Englewood Cliffs, N.J.: Prentice-Hall, 1966), part IV.
Tibor Scitovsky, *The Joyless Economy* (New York: Oxford University Press, 1976).

Chapter 1

Temptation

My wife Nancy, who smokes more than a pack a day, never buys cigarettes by the carton. She continually runs out and is often forced to purchase from vending machines, paying some 30 percent more per pack than necessary. She argues that possessing few cigarettes helps her ration them, that if there were always some lying around the house she would smoke more, which would be worse, and that her behavior makes sense.

Nancy's desire to limit the number of cigarettes in the house is an attempt to reduce temptation. A temptation situation is defined here as one in which a person must make a choice between two alternatives; one alternative is less valuable but more immediate or specific, while the other is more valuable, but more remote or abstract.[1] Nancy's behavior is designed to increase the cost of the first alternative. Embarking on a vacation deep in the wilds without cigarettes could be considered a strategic maneuver aimed at virtually eliminating the choice.[2]

It is well known that in a two-or-more-person game, a player can be made better off by actually worsening certain of his payoffs. (The appendix provides a simple introduction for those not familiar with payoff matrices.) Consider the single prisoner's dilemma game below (figure 1-1) with no communication or side payments. Each player has a dominant strategy, to choose option A regardless of the other's choice. Individual maximizing behavior will give the players a payoff of three each. Now if certain payoffs could be *worsened*, the outcome of rational individualistic behavior can be improved. In the revised game depicted in figure 1-2, option B has become the dominant strat-

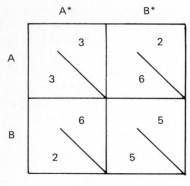

Figure 1-1.

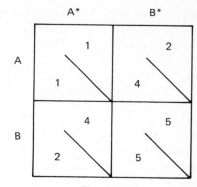

Figure 1-2.

egy, and payoffs of five each are obtained. The argument here is that even in one-person games, games with no externalities, worsening payoffs or eliminating options can sometimes make the player better off. Conversely, adding options or improving payoffs can actually worsen the ultimate outcome.

There are a number of possible reasons why having additional choices might actually decrease one's utility. These include the costs of comprehension and calculation, and the higher disutility of making the wrong decision (and crying over spilt milk) rather than having no decision to make at all. This chapter focuses on a somewhat different explanation, the problem of shorter-run vs. longer-run benefits, of shorter-run vs. longer-run rationality, the problem of temptation.

For temptation to matter in the economic model, the assumption of complete rationality must be modified. More realistically, people are less rational and make worse decisions in the immediate or short run, when, perhaps, they haven't had time to "sleep on it." The explanation is not that they have less information (though this is certainly possible), but that their utility calculus is less reliable. Given more time, for example, they often have longer (and more correct) time horizons. Being able to step back and examine the situation in its totality, they become less myopic.

Considering the example of Nancy and her cigarettes, we have in some respects a situation of shifting controls, actually a two-person game. It makes sense for one Nancy, who has had a chance to carefully weigh all alternatives, to change payoffs or eliminate options for another Nancy, who must make quick decisions in the face of immediate temptation.

Businesses understand and try to capitalize on the shorter-run irrationality of consumers. "Impulse purchases" account for an important part of supermarket sales, and firms use packaging and display techniques as well as "magic prices" (generally with a 9¢ ending) to increase particular sales.[3] Recognizing the more emotional and impulsive nature of snap judgments, sellers sometimes try to force instant decisions on buyers. It is in this light that such promotions as "The first twenty callers will receive free . . ." or "Offer expires midnight tonight" can be viewed. One purpose of the recent buyer remorse law allowing a three-day "cooling-off" period during which households may legally renege on a door-to-door sales agreement is to help consumers combat the problem of spontaneous irrational purchase.

Individual consumers have various devices for combatting temptation. Nancy's refusal to buy cigarette cartons has already been discussed. Those trying to cut down on food or alcohol usually have their own little games. Women on diets, for example, often buy clothes too small as an incentive to lose weight. Some have actually gone so far as to get their jaws wired shut. A number of my friends don't own television sets, largely, I suspect, because they are afraid they will watch too much. Their longer-run actions prevent short-run mistakes. Sometimes I believe I might be better off if excellent diversions were not located so close to my office.

People combat the short-run temptation to spend money in a variety of ways. Some take only a limited amount to the track or the gambling casino in order to avoid too large losses. Potential purchasers sometimes avoid attending auctions in person to prevent the excitement of the competitive bidding from driving their offers too high. Certain institutions and commercial successes are explicable, I believe, largely in terms of helping consumers delay gratification, in helping them refrain from current consumption. If one were knowledgeable, and always rational, there would be little reason, for example, to prefer whole life to term insurance. But recognizing the irrationality of some short-run decisions, one may be afraid of extra money "lying around the house" "burning a hole in one's pocket," and correctly opt for the forced saving in the whole life policy, even if the interest rate is low. This also accounts for the popularity of low-interest Christmas Club plans and is a major argument for the withholding of taxes.

There are many general examples of actions designed in part to diminish the effect of short-run temptation. Collectively, Americans prohibit the three-term president and often prevent governors from succeeding themselves, thus eliminating a seemingly important option. On the Golden Gate Bridge, expensive railing may be installed to stop additional suicides. Even the awful seat-belt buzzer can be

partly defended as a device that helps prevent the short-run temptation "to forget it this one time" from winning out over the longer-
run calculation of the dangers of driving.

It may make some sense for the government to help individuals
combat temptation when the problem is general and there are scale
economies or when it is individually difficult to make firm commitments. Partial justification can be made on such grounds for the
mandatory seat belt, and perhaps the restriction on cigarette ads.
(The argument for governmental intervention could also be made in
terms of externalities. In the case of, say, gun control or social-
security legislation, it is this, rather than the temptation rationale,
that is perhaps persuasive.) This kind of public action is, of course,
fraught with danger. Rarely do we *all* want particular payoffs worsened or options eliminated. Collective deliverance from temptation,
for example, is one rationale for such problem laws as prohibition
and the illegality of prostitution and pornography. It is significant,
however, that these laws are generally felt to be legitimate when
applied to minors, who do not yet possess sufficient "long-run
rationality" to look out for themselves.

People often attempt to help those "less rational" to resist temptation. For example, the appointment of a financial trustee to take
care of the estate after death is one way a husband can continue to
protect "the little woman." A mother who desires to safeguard her
daughter's virtue may refuse to provide birth-control pills. She is
afraid of condoning promiscuity and actually wants to worsen the
payoffs of such behavior. There are dangers here, as in all the examples, of the individual's still finding temptation irresistible and paying
more dearly. While this chapter has focused on worsening outcomes,
it is obvious that the preferred strategy may sometimes be to improve
payoffs in order to lower the costs of succumbing to temptation.

Temptation has been narrowly defined here. It has not been
viewed as "an invitation to evil," an attempt to cheat or steal and
thus to harm others. Instead it has been described as an "invitation"
to do something—anything—that brings immediate, often tangible
personal utility, but is against one's own long-term interest. The
essay ignored many tempting topics such as morality, conscience,
will, guilt, and the superego.[4] There has been no mention of the
potential character-building benefits of being tempted, the potential
costs of rationality, or the joys of unfettered spontaneity. The argument has been the simple one that economists should recognize different degrees of rationality and that these may be related to the
time of and for decision. While we are being immediately tempted,
we often give long-run consequences too little weight and are enticed
to do things we later regret. It thus sometimes makes sense for us to

create schemes that eliminate particular options, or at least make them less attractive. Certain of our actions and institutions are explicable as ways we help ourselves combat the dangers of temptation.

FOR DISCUSSION

1. "Consumer theory doesn't explain addictive goods too well." Comment. Is there any difference between the utility derivable from addictive goods and normal goods? What type of goods are addictive? Can man ever become addicted to comforts? to status? to making money? to consumption in general?

2. Both buyer and seller should benefit from free trade. Did American Indians benefit from the purchase of white man's firewater? Why might they not have?

3. What is meant by the saying: "He is his own worst enemy"? Is rational man ever his own worst enemy?

4. Do you ever play games with yourself, or try to fool yourself for your long-term well-being? In what kinds of situations?

5. Why do people sometimes count to ten before reacting to another's objectionable behavior?

6. "Never go grocery shopping when you're hungry." Comment.

7. Why are children warned against snacks that might "spoil their appetite"? What is meant by a person being spoiled?

8. How would you go about collecting empirical evidence on temptation?

9. List a number of areas where it might make sense for government to help people resist temptation. Could laws against prostitution or bottomless dancers ever be justified on this rationale? How about fines for not locking your car, "tempting" people to steal it? What would be the benefits and costs of government's banning TV broadcasting for one hour each night?

10. Are there any cultural activities you were forced into, somewhat against your will, which you have now grown quite fond of? Relate such situations to temptation situations.

NOTES TO CHAPTER ONE

1. Robert Grinder, "Behavior in a Temptation Situation and Its Relation to Certain Aspects of Socialization," Harvard Ph.D. thesis in psychology, 1960.

2. Thomas C. Schelling, *The Strategy of Conflict* (New York: Oxford University Press, 1963), p. 123.

3. Hearings before the House Interstate and Foreign Commerce Committee on the Fair Labelling and Packaging Act, 89th Cong., 2nd sess. (1966), pp. 1064, 1093.

4. Carole Friedman Gilligan, "Responses to Temptation: An Analysis of Motives," Harvard Ph.D. thesis in psychology, 1963.

※ *Chapter 2*

Options

Gaining additional options is usually thought advantageous. More alternatives are generally considered to be
better than fewer alternatives. One is deemed fortunate
to have a large choice in deciding where to work, or what to buy,
or whom to marry. But an increase in options is not always an un-
mixed blessing. In some areas additional alternatives may have
detrimental rather than beneficial effects.

SOCIAL PERSPECTIVE

Economists have long understood that increasing the discretionary
power of individual decision-makers may harm society. Competition is viewed as beneficial largely because it limits such power on
the part of firms. In the model of perfect competition, sellers are
forced to produce where price equals marginal cost, and their actions
help lead to a Pareto optimal equilibrium. Possessing market power
increases the firm's options, but generally decreases the economic
efficiency and well-being of the society. We don't want the firm to
be able to continually charge monopoly prices and prosper. Thus, we
have regulatory agencies that limit the pricing options of natural
monopolies. There is a potential rationale for some sort of regulation
whenever markets are imperfect. For example, insufficient consumer
information is sometimes cited as creating a need for our usury, fair-
packaging, and pure-food laws whose purpose is to eliminate supposedly undesirable or unneeded alternatives.

Efficiency problems are also caused by externalities. Where there are substantial external economies, where social exceed private benefits, it may behoove society to bolster or subsidize the activities. On the other hand, where there are substantial external diseconomies, it may be appropriate government policy to try to curtail them. In the real world it sometimes makes sense to outlaw rather than tax certain of these activities, so we have traffic laws, zoning codes, effluent controls, etc. Of course, making particular alternatives unlawful merely eliminates *legal* options. The course of action may still be possible, but it is made more costly by potential moral problems, court expenses, fines, jail sentences, etc.

We have limited the legal options concerning printing money, paying taxes, immigrating, discriminating, and selling our liquor, our votes, or our bodies. We may eventually want to eliminate the legal option of killing baby whales, or carrying handguns, or having too many children. And if we discover how to choose our children's genes, we may want to limit or control that option. Or we may not.[1]

INDIVIDUAL PERSPECTIVE

Up to now we have been considering options that we as individuals might be willing to relinquish if others also gave up those alternatives. For example, we probably want automobile speed limits, provided they are applicable to most or all vehicles, not just our own. There are other options we might not want for ourselves, independent of whether or not they are made available to others.

In the model of perfect competition, where everyone is perfectly rational and perfectly informed and where it is costless to make commitments, additional independent options (options that do not affect the payoffs to other alternatives) should not prove harmful. In the real world, however, extra alternatives are sometimes troublesome or detrimental.

It is obvious that additional undesirable options can prove detrimental when they directly worsen payoffs to other alternatives. The employee may not want the option of spending a dull evening at his boss's house, or having an affair with the boss's spouse. The teenager may not want the option of taking speed with his buddies. A Frank Serpico did not want the alternative of making easy money through graft. For the individual, the option may not be agreeable, but not taking it now has added costs: he may lose face or his job, his friends, his life.

Additional options that don't directly worsen a man's payoffs may nonetheless affect others' *expectations* concerning his actions and thus make him worse off. It is well known that in game theoretic situations, increased payoffs or additional alternatives can actually worsen results. A legal option of selling your vote may make you more susceptible to intimidation. An army's ability to retreat may make the feared enemy attack more likely. One's newfound tolerance and willingness to compromise may make others more strident in their demands.[2]

Even a decision unit viewed in isolation may prefer fewer options.

1. There is disutility in having had a choice and making the wrong one. Of course, we may be unhappy with the added option if we chose it and things turned out badly. But there is more than this. Having an alternative and making the wrong choice is usually worse than reaching the same outcome having had no choice at all. Psychologically, bygones are not simply bygones, and we do tend to cry over spilt milk. The utility of the present situation is decreased by the unfavorable comparison to what could have been. In addition, the wrong selection may make us unhappy by reflecting badly on our rationality, intelligence, and shrewdness. To protect ourselves we sometimes try, ex post, to change our beliefs. We try to increase the attractiveness of the chosen alternative and to decrease the attractiveness of the rejected. This opposite of "the grass is greener" syndrome is called the theory of cognitive dissonance reduction[3] and is well known in market research literature. We try to reduce dissonance because past, unchosen alternatives *do* affect our present contentment.

2. Decisions take time, and time is a scarce resource. The thinking required for the decision may be hard. Information about alternatives is often fragmentary, and there is cost in gaining more information. There are costs in determining one's own preferences, one's own utility function. If the decision unit is a group, a family for instance, it may be difficult to determine the intensity of each member's desires and somehow correctly to weigh those desires. (Furthermore, family members' expectations may be changed, perhaps detrimentally, by the new option.) The decision-maker can try to optimize which choices to consider and how much to consider them, but there can clearly be many options he can very well do without. Take a seemingly favorable opportunity: the family breadwinner is offered a slightly better job, but in a different city. Whatever alternative is chosen and whatever the outcome, there can certainly be large psychic and emotional costs in the decision-making process itself. One can easily imagine that the family might have been better off without such a potentially difficult choice.

Some psychiatrists claim that too many attractive options can lead to psychic overload. As affluence increases, as customs and mores lose their stability, we may enter a state that could be termed "option-shock." To quote Dr. Lipowski:

It is specifically the overabundance of attractive alternatives, aided and abetted by an affluent and increasingly complex society, that leads to conflict, frustration, unrelieved appetitive tension, more approach tendencies, and more conflict—a veritable vicious cycle. Such an overload and its consequences constitute a category of psychosocial stress that must have far-reaching and probably harmful effects on the mental and physical health of affected individuals.[4]

3. Individuals may just not act rationally. They may be inexperienced, intoxicated, insane, incensed, in too dire straits. Society, for example, tries to prevent the young from becoming addicted to cigarettes. Society eliminates even more options for the insane. Sometimes normal adults may simply be too weak in the face of temptation to respond rationally in the short run. A woman on a diet, for instance, may strongly prefer *not* to be offered a piece of delicious chocolate cream pie. She is probably better off without the option.

CONCLUSION

As individuals, we often like to limit others' options, especially as they affect us, and we are sometimes willing to limit our own to achieve this purpose. But independent of limitations on others, there are also many occasions when we would prefer not to have additional, even alluring, alternatives. Our added options may change others' expectations in an adverse manner. And even a Robinson Crusoe may prefer fewer options if he suspects he may choose wrongly, if a wrong choice makes him feel terrible, or if the act of choosing is itself traumatic.

FOR DISCUSSION

1. Why do many people dislike face-to-face encounters with individuals seeking charitable contributions? Will "not-giving" convey a bad signal or create a bad impression? Is it ever rational to pretend you're not at home when a neighbor comes collecting?

2. Do you ever try to make it impossible to do things you don't want to do?

3. J.J. Rousseau said: "If in order to fall heir to the property of a rich mandarin living at the farthest confines of China, whom one had never seen or heard spoken of, it were enough to push a button to make him die, which of us would not push that button?" Would you want such an option?

4. "One of the reasons for having a book of rules about when to run the risk and when not to—when to land the disabled aircraft and when to abandon it and take to parachute—is to relieve the man who gives the orders, the man in the control tower, of personal guilt for the instruction he gives."[5] Discuss in relation to the Rousseau quote above. Could possible guilt feelings be considered a completely separate and additional reason for not wanting options?

5. "In matters of life and death doctors are not merely operations analysts who formulate the choice for the executive; they are professional decision makers, who not only diagnose but decide for the consumer, because they decide with less pain, less regret, cooler nerves, and a mind less flooded with alternating hopes and fears."[6] Comment.

6. Contrast the tendency to cry over spilt milk with the economist's advice that sunk costs are sunk, to let bygones be bygones.

7. Can the existence of an option be detrimental even if there is no possibility of a wrong choice? Explain.

8. Is there an "optimal amount of options"? Is that a useful concept? Is the actual amount of options generally less than the optimal amount?

NOTES TO CHAPTER TWO

1. Thomas C. Schelling, "Hockey Helmets, Concealed Weapons, and Daylight Saving" *Journal of Conflict Resolution,* 17; no. 3 (September 1973); "On the Ecology of Micromotives," *The Public Interest,* no. 25 (Fall 1971); "Choosing Our Children's Genes," Harvard Institute of Economic Research, Discussion Paper No. 304 (June 1973).

2. Thomas C. Schelling, *The Strategy of Conflict* (New York: Oxford University Press paper, 1963).

3. Robert Holloway, Robert Mittelstaedt, M. Venkatesan, eds. *Consumer Behavior: Contemporary Research in Action* (Boston: Houghton-Mifflin, 1971).

4. Z.J. Lipowski, "The Conflict of Buridan's Ass or Some Dilemmas of Affluence: The Theory of Attractive Stimulus Overload," *American Journal of Psychiatry* 127, no. 3 (September 1970).

5. Thomas C. Schelling, "The Life You Save May Be Your Own," in Samuel B. Chase, ed., *Problems in Public Expenditure Analysis* (Washington: Brookings Institute, 1968), p. 130.

6. Ibid., p. 147.

Chapter 3

Fashion

Expenditure for display is more obviously present, and is, perhaps
more universally practiced in the matter of dress than in any
other line of consumption. . . . The greater part of the expenditure incurred by all classes for apparel is incurred for the sake of a respect-
able appearance rather than for the protection of the person. And probably
at no other point is the sense of shabbiness so keenly felt as it is if we fall
short of the standard set by social usage in this matter of dress. . . . People
will undergo a very considerable degree of privation in the comforts or the
necessities of life in order to afford what is considered a decent amount of
wasteful consumption; so that it is by no means an uncommon occurrence,
in an inclement climate, for people to go ill clad in order to appear well
dressed. And the ceremonial value of the goods used for clothing in any
modern community is made up to a much larger extent of the fashionable-
ness, the reputability of the goods than the mechanical service which they
render in clothing the person of the wearer.[1]

There are fads and fashions in many areas: architecture, automo-
biles, pets, games, psychology, even diseases. Why do fashions in
clothing change, and what are the effects of such change on economic well-being?

Clothing protects, but also decorates, the body. Most of the
expenditure on clothes is undoubtedly for display purposes. Clothing
is intimately connected with personal presentation, and thus ultimately connected with role playing and social rankings. This means, in
economic jargon, that there are strong externalities in this field of
consumption.

Externalities exist because what others wear dramatically affects the utility we receive from any particular item of clothing we possess. What (certain) others wear in large part determines what is fashionable, what is presentable, and even what we think fits well. While most people are not bound by fashion, all are influenced by it.

An expert on marketing and fashion writes:

> If any reader of this should doubt the power of fashion, let him try a simple experiment and note his own reactions. Let him put on clothes as worn by a past generation and then go out as casually as he can among his acquaintances or in fact among strangers and note, first, their reactions toward him and then his feelings toward himself. There will be quizzical looks, doubtful stares and critical estimates. He will be thought queer. He will be judged as lacking in brain power and, perhaps, as an undesirable person. If he persists in his experiment, he will, if he is an employee, lose his job. He will lose his customers if he is a salesman. He will lose votes if he is a politician. . . . No man can belong to present-day society and at the same time be completely out of present-day fashions.[2]

THE PURSUIT OF STATUS

Most people feel the need and desire to conform to the prevailing styles. However, if conformity were the only motive behind dress, there would be little need for a theory of changing fashion; dress styles might tend to be relatively fixed. What-to-wear would be a cooperative game, reaching a stable equilibrium once acceptable custom was established.

But there are usually other social motives behind clothing. The most important of these is the attempt to gain prestige, the desire to help insure or improve one's ranking on some status hierarchy. The material goods most closely associated with the ego are often clothes, with fashion serving "as an outward emblem of personal distinction or of membership in some group to which distinction is ascribed."[3] This desire for distinction and prestige is a crucial cause of the volatility of fashion in a dynamic society.

Status is a relative rather than an absolute concept. In terms of status alone, the competition for prestige has characteristics similar to a zero-sum game. One individual or group gains only at the expense of another. This means that for goods consumed principally for status rather than functional utility, social and economic welfare need not be enhanced by increased production. More of the good is not necessarily better than less of it.

For the economist, "goods"—as opposed to "bads" like pollution or garbage—are generally assumed to bring direct functional utility. An apple can nourish us, satisfy our appetite, and taste delicious.

This is an economic good with economic value because it is scarce, because everyone cannot have as much as he desires. Costlessly increasing the supply fo such a good, for example, through technological advance, may lower its relative price, but it should increase material well-being.

Pure prestige items, on the other hand, are valued not for their functional utility, but principally *because* they are scarce or rare.[4] Increasing the supply of a status good not only tends to decrease its price, but also to lower the actual prestige benefits provided by previous units. For example, much of the pleasure to be derived from ownership of an original Picasso print comes from the prestige it engenders. A virtually perfect copy, aesthetically as pleasing, is not nearly so valuable. Limiting the number of original prints, especially by the destruction of the lithograph, may be sound business policy, but it initially seems economically wasteful. Yet increasing production, or even discovering more originals, may not provide much social benefit. At least in terms of prestige, while new owners advance in status, they do so only as others retreat.

In *Essays in Persuasion*, John Maynard Keynes briefly mentions that class of wants "which are relative in the sense that we feel them only if their satisfaction lifts us above, makes us feel superior to, our fellows. Needs of [this] second class, those which satisfy the desire for superiority, may indeed be insatiable, for the higher the general level, the higher still they are."[5] While John Kenneth Galbraith might extend the argument, he would heartily agree that when goods satisfy only status needs, more output is not necessarily socially beneficial. "In technical terms, it can no longer be assumed that welfare is greater at an all-around higher level of production than at a lower one. It may be the same."[6]

SUMPTUOSITY

The argument thus far has been that where goods provide status and prestige, there are negative externalities in consumption. Now most goods and services probably furnish both prestige and functional utility (as well as other possible benefits). With respect to clothing, prestige is generally the more important of the two. All social scientists agree that the key motivation behind most expenditures for bodily adornment is display rather than protection.

There are many reasons, most of them social, why an individual wears specific types of clothes. In terms of identification alone, clothes can help group us by age, sex, occupation, marital standing, or team membership. Clothing may also demonstrate our economic status, and it is upon this aspect of fashion that Thorstein Veblen focuses.

Veblen argues that "in order to gain and hold the esteem of men it is not sufficient merely to possess wealth or power. The wealth or power must be put in evidence."[7] The choice of clothing is often crucial for the display of purchasing power. Expenditures for dress are important for pecuniary repute since "our apparel is always in evidence and affords an indication of our pecuniary standing to all observers at first glance."[8] Fashion is an ideal arena for "conspicuous consumption," lavish expenditure that satisfies no real need, but is merely a mark of socioeconomic status. Hence the sumptuousness of much of our clothing, especially formal attire.

Veblen emphasizes not only conspicuous consumption in bringing reputability, but also the related conspicuousness of leisure. While the poor are economically forced to perform productive, often physical work, the rich are not. Thus, historically, abstention from labor was often an indication of great wealth, and the display of leisure became valued as a mark of high social standing. Therefore, says Veblen, for dress to promote status, it "should be expensive, but it should also make plain to all observers that the wearer is not engaged in any kind of productive labor," that he or she is not under the necessity of earning a livelihood.[9]

Elegant apparel, Veblen argues, is contrived at every point to signal that the wearer does not habitually put forth any useful effort. "The pleasing effect of neat and spotless garments is chiefly, if not altogether, due to their carrying the suggestion of leisure—exemption from personal contact with industrial processes of any kind."[10] Linen has been especially useful for both conspicuous consumption and leisure, for it betrays dirt at once and must be frequently renewed.[11]

Veblen explains the corset, the dress, and high heels among women as forms of conspicuous leisure, demonstration of an honorably futile existence, one that is so far removed from menial necessities that clothes can be worn that actually impede physical labor. Similarly, refined tastes and manners are useful evidence of gentility, because good breeding requires time and expense. "A knowledge of good form is prima facie evidence that that portion of a well-bred person's life which is not spent under observation of the spectator has been worthily spent in acquiring accomplishments that are of no lucrative effect."[12]

Like "good" manners, "correct" attire is determined socially rather than individually. Many consumers may correctly argue that the principles of conspicuous consumption and leisure do not directly motivate their individual purchases. Their wish is merely "to conform to established usage, to avoid unfavorable notice and comment, to live up to the accepted canons of decency in the kind, amount and grade of goods consumed, as well as in the decorous employment of their time and effort."[13] Yet is is precisely these rules of proper and responsible behavior that Veblen argues are basically molded by the competition for status and the norm of conspicuous waste.

AESTHETIC PERCEPTION

Society not only dictates what is correct and proper, but also influences what is considered aesthetic and beautiful. The prevailing fashion, for example, clearly affects our tastes. Clothes that were yesterday so attractive often seem today to have lost their aesthetic as well as social appeal. As a professor of marketing writes:

> The influence of fashion over the human mind is such as to make a style, when accepted, seem beautiful, no matter how hideous it may appear at other times when not in fashion. It is hard to believe that the hoop skirt, the bustle and the leg o'mutton sleeve were once considered very charming and highly appropriate. No doubt the present fashions will in time seem just as ridiculous and even, probably, as hideous as do those past styles seem now.[14]

Veblen argues that pecuniary criteria often underlie aesthetic judgments of what is considered appealing and what becomes fashionable. Costliness, he says, often masquerades as beauty. Fancy-bred dogs are considered aesthetic, primarily because of their expense. Conversely, beautiful flowers often are labeled common weeds, because of their cheapness. Handmade items, even with marked imperfections and irregularities, are presently judged superior to machine woven, because of their relative prices. Similarly, natural fibers are becoming increasingly admired relative to man-made fabric.

When women were valued for their service, as in Homeric times, the ideal female was robust and large-limbed. Today, the identification of repute with conspicuous leisure has made the delicate face, the slender figure, and the constricted waist hallmarks of beauty. When female physical labor often meant fieldwork under the hot sun, paleness was admired. Presently, with most women working indoors, it is the suntanned look that has gained wide acceptance. In China, the deformed feet of the female, the "golden lilies," were a mark of both conspicuous leisure and sexual appeal.

Aesthetics matter a great deal for display items such as clothing. If pecuniary values do affect aesthetic (as well as snob) appeal, this may have important implications for welfare analysis. While economists, perhaps wisely, are generally loath to deal in intertemporal as well as interpersonal utility comparisons, let us venture very briefly into this treacherous terrain.

Assume that technological improvements allow our society to have, ceteris paribus, more fur coats. In time, as they become more common, will they not only be less desirable for prestige and status purposes, but actually feel less soft, look less lovely, smell less heavenly? If so, increased production will not make society as materially better off as might initially be supposed. However, an offsetting factor would be if those goods becoming relatively more scarce, for instance, cloth coats, began to increase in aesthetic appeal. (The introduction of new goods further complicates the analysis.)

FASHION

Veblen's theory of conspicuous consumption and leisure appears useful in explaining much of the sumptuosity of wearing apparel. This is true not only for dynamic societies, but also for those communities where styles have remained largely static. The dress of the upper class in ancient China, for example, seems designed to display the leisure life. The long silk robe of the mandarin with its projecting sleeves served well to frustrate any attempts at manual labor. Similarly, the scholar's habit of allowing fingernails to grow to prodigious lengths advertised mental rather than physical exertion.[15]

Fashion—the rapidly changing vogues in clothing styles—is explained in large part by the constant *competition* for status. Such competition assumes the ability to rise in status—and to use clothing as a symbol and weapon in the endeavor. The status competition may be within, or between, classes or groups, though historically interclass competition appears the more important. When there was no upward social mobility, where class was unalterable, society and clothing styles also tended to be static.

In feudal society, with its traditional stratification systems, the little fashion consciousness that existed resided primarily within the upper class and seems caused by intraclass status rivalry. The ceilings placed on the upward mobility of the lower classes decreased their individual distinctiveness in dress; folk costume existed rather than continual fashion change. It was when the economy became more dynamic and the social order began to disintegrate, increasing the possibility of social advance, that fashion came into its own.

As individuals from lower social groupings attempt to ascend the status hierarchy, they naturally tend to imitate the behavior and attire of those above. A psychologist writes:

> So long as a system of "fixed" custom prevails, each social grade is content to wear the costume with which it is associated. But when the barriers between one grade and another become less insuperable, when, in psychological terms, one class begins to aspire to the position above it, it is natural that the distinctive outward signs and symbols of the grades in question should become imperilled. . . . it is a fundamental human trait to imitate those who are admired or envied . . . and what more natural, and, at the same time, more symbolic, than to start the process of imitation by copying their clothes, the very insignia of the admired and envied qualities?[16]

In order to maintain their own distinctiveness, members of the upper class are forced to change their mode of dress. Eventually, a new upper-class style of attire emerges and this in turn is copied. This process—fashion—can continue endlessly, the highest class trying to differentiate itself, the lower classes in hot pursuit. As William Hazlitt wrote in 1818: "(Fashion) is a continual struggle between 'the great vulgar and the small' to get the start of, or keep up with each other in the race of appearance."[17] Since the upper class tends to desert a fashion as soon as it spreads widely, it is often said that a successful fashion sows the seeds of its own destruction.

Status rivalries are one explanation for the *continuing* change in clothing styles. Styles, of course, may change at any time for a wide variety of other reasons. The general mode of dress may be modified by the introduction of new materials or new ideas; it may be affected by government decree or climatic changes, by changes in people's activities or changes in relative prices. Clothing styles could thus change with some frequency even where class structure was rigid and consumers noncompetitive.

Speed of Fashion Change
The mode of dress is but one aspect and reflection of the whole culture. The art, music, manners, morals, ideas, the work and play of the society, all tend to influence what clothes people wear. As these factors change, so might we expect clothing to change. The more dynamic the society, the more it changes, probably the more rapid will be the changes in clothing styles.

In terms of the competition for status, styles should change more rapidly the faster they are spread. And over time in Western society, followers have become quicker in emulating the leaders owing to the increase in living standards of the poor, the general improvements in communication and transportation, and to such specific inventions as sewing machines and man-made fibers that have made it possible to imitate the current vogue quickly and cheaply.

As Western society advanced and became more dynamic, fashions changed more rapidly. Nineteenth-century clothes, writes fashion author Jane Dorner,

> changed more often than they had in all the previous five centuries. This constant variety was due in some measure to the fact that fashions were becoming available to a wider range of people, with the result that the upper classes were constantly seeking novelty in a bid to retain their social superiority.[18]

Another factor tending to increase the speed of style change has been growing urbanization. Urban areas have always been more fashion conscious than rural areas, in part because of the anonymity of city life, which increases the significance of symbolic display. Moreover, an urban environment multiplies the number of face-to-face encounters and thus quickens the general spread of fashion information. The growth of the cities undoubtedly contributed to the growing importance and increasing speed of style change.

Laws can be used to affect the spread of fashion and the speed of style change. The upper class does not always run away from its sartorial pursuers. It sometimes tries to stop them. During the thirteenth and fourteenth centuries, for example, the number of sumptuary laws increased dramatically as the landed gentry attempted to stop the sartorial imitations of the urban middle class.[19] England's King Edward III decreed that a man could not dress above his station:

> All esquires and every gentleman under the estate of knighthood, and not possessed of lands or tenements to the yearly amount of 200 marks, shall use in their dress such cloth as does not exceed the value of 4 marks and a half the whole cloth; they shall not wear any cloth of gold, or silk, or of silver, nor any sort of embroidered garment, nor any ring, buckle, nouche, riband nor girdle; nor any ornaments of precious stones, nor furs of any kind; their wives and children shall be subject to the same regulation.[20]

Sumptuary laws generally prove ineffective in the long run; in the short run, however, they may have some impact. Recently, for example, while dealing more with moral than status concerns, sumptuary laws regulating bathing costumes probably helped prevent the spread of the topless swimsuit phenomenon.

Some Effects of Fashion

Fads, such as Hula-Hoops, backgammon, or house plants, can spring up independent of a predecessor, and may give rise to no successor. They have no line of historical continuity.[21] Fashion change, on the other hand, is evolutionary, gradual rather than abrupt. While an individual may try to distinguish himself with his attire, he is also required to largely conform to the prevailing sartorial norm. Otherwise he will appear ridiculous. Styles therefore tend to change only at the margin. Skirt lengths, for example, may move up and down, but slowly, not radically. Similarly, hair styles may get longer or shorter, but quantum leaps are unlikely.

Fashion change is large enough, of course, to make the old style look old and outmoded. Unfortunately, most fashion change does not represent an improvement; each new fashion is not aesthetically more pleasing than its predecessor once seemed, nor more comfortable or functional. While there is sartorial evolution, there is no clear upward progression.

Fashion may provide some utility to those people who enjoy and prefer to live in a society of flux and change. There are those who delight in the competitiveness of fashion, and those who are good at predicting new trends can clearly benefit from changing styles. But for the average person, fashion is primarily a significant, though familiar burden.

> The average consumer is chronically distressed to discover how rapidly his accumulated property in wear depreciates by becoming outmoded. He complains bitterly and ridicules the new fashions when they (first) appear. In the end he succumbs, a victim to symbolisms of behavior which he does not fully comprehend. What he will never admit is that he is more the creator than the victim of his difficulties.[22]

Fashion is an outgrowth of the pursuit of status. While competitive consumption could theoretically result in a single, constant, but increasingly sumptuous style, in the real world it has meant ever-changing fashion. In either situation, the social costs, while not identical, are broadly similar. The average individual is continually forced into additional expenditures for items that buy little additional functional utility, but only help him to remain in the same status position.

Fashion Anecdotes

There are a large number of stories and anecdotes about fashion that lend support to some of the arguments in the text, give a glimpse of the fascinating variety of historical clothing styles, and, most of all, are inherently interesting. Here are a few:[23]

Function or Display? It was cold, and the tribesman of Tierra del Fuego wore no clothes. So Charles Darwin gave him a large piece of red cloth. Did the native wrap it around him? Not exactly. He immediately tore the cloth into strips and distributed these among his friends, who tied them round their arms and legs as adornment.

Fashion Leadership. The hiatus in English fashion that accompanied the Puritan reign of Oliver Cromwell was ended with the return of Charles II. Charles had spent much of his time in exile at the court of Louis XIV, and brought back with him many of the latest French modes. But some rivalry existed between monarchs, and this was increased by Charles's attempts to break the French dictatorship over fashion. Charles's most significant innovation was a half-length coat, called a "vest," the forerunner of the kind later worn by all eighteenth-century gentlemen. The vest was described by John Evelyn in his diary of 18 October 1666: "It being the first time his Majesty put himself into the eastern fashion of vest, changing doublet, stiff collar, bands and cloak into a comely dress after the Persian mode, with girdles or straps, and shoestrings and garters into buckles, of which some are set with precious stones."

Louis, the Sun King, to show his superiority in matters of fashion decided to mock Charles's attempts at fashion leadership. How? Louis had all his footmen, and only his footmen, wear Charles's newfangled "vest." This made Samuel Pepys "mighty merry, it being an ingenious kind of affront."

Style Evolution. Trousers for women made their debut in America in 1849 with the Rational Dress Campaign of Amelia Jenks Bloomer. The "Bloomer costume" was a cross between a pair of cossacks and long knickerbockers, with a short skirt modestly worn over the top as a concession to convention. Although Amelia crisscrossed the country lecturing on its advantages, the bloomer had little initial success. The idea was too far ahead of its time. However, some thirty years later, when bicycling became a feminine pastime, the bloomer gained wide acceptance.

As Ada Ballin wrote in *The Science of Dress:*

> The feeling against the Bloomer costume was very strong, for although it had many good points about it, it represented too violent a change from the fashion of the time and ladies would not adopt it for fear of appearing

ridiculous. Reform to be effective must be gradual, and it takes some time for the public to become accustomed to a new idea even in dress.

At the same time the bloomer became acceptable, the bustle lost its appeal. The bustle was a pad worn under the skirt to swell the fullness of the rear end. The bustle made it difficult to stand upright, awkward to walk, and positively dangerous to sit down. Bicycling is credited not only with popularizing the bloomer, but also with destroying the bustle.

Sports do not aways hold the upper hand to fashion, however. Though roller skating, or "rinking," was quite popular among women in the late nineteenth century, as skirts grew tighter in the 1870s and 1880s, skating became impossible and had to be temporarily abandoned to await the advent of the looser Edwardian styles. Female tennis also suffered fashion difficulties. Stiff corseted clothes were common on the courts until champion Suzanne Lenglen shocked Wimbledon in 1922 by appearing in a "short" (midcalf) skirt. Ten years later, on the same courts, Alice Marble astonished the world by appearing in shorts! Many people thought this was going really too far for the sake of the game.

Fashion Extravagances. Styles often tend to the extreme. We have witnessed this in our own era, with the stiletto heel for women and the micro-mini dress. Other examples: In the 1880s the bustle had reached such an extent that it jutted out like a shelf "whereon a good-sized tea tray might be carried." During the reign of Louis XVI, hair styles had grown to such a degree that Marie Antoinette (known for her taste and elegance) had a coiffure that rose thirty-six inches above her head. And in the 1550s, the bodice for a time became so deep cut as to expose the nipples.

Men, who have often been more style conscious than women, have also had their style extremes. In the 1550s fashionable trousers became so stuffed with rich materials that a scandalized German Protestant church placed the "trouser devil" into its list of devils. A century earlier, before the advent of stocking-pants, fashionable coats became so short that when a man bent over he exposed his bare posterior. An English sumptuary law, passed in 1475 proclaimed: "Nobody below the rank of Lord, Esquire, or Gentleman may wear a coat, cape or smock so short that when he stands erect it fails to cover his private parts and buttocks, in which case he pays a fine of twenty shillings." The privilege of exposing oneself in public was thereby reserved for the upper classes.

Deleterious Fashion. We are often shocked and bemused by such savage customs as the filing down of front teeth, the flattening of foreheads, or the plate-shaping of the lips. These and other forms of self-mutilation are performed for religious reasons (teeth are filed to permit free passage of the soul), to demonstrate abstention from physical labor (the elongated head indicates that heavy burdens cannot be carried there), and for other motives such as the practical one of avoiding slavery (a female with distorted lips is less in danger of being kidnapped for concubinage).

We should not forget, however, that Western man, primarily through his fashions, has also disfigured and deformed his own body. He has focused his attention principally on the waist and on the feet.

Most shoe styles restrict and deform the foot. They are thus deleterious to the health. High heels are among the worst, leading to podiatric disorders, calf muscle shortening, sway back, etc. The constriction of the waist by corsets and girdles causes even more serious medical problems. Circulation and breathing are impeded, creating all sorts of difficulties from anemia to headaches to fainting spells. A shrinking of the rib cage also increases pressure on the internal organs; additional troubles are caused and compounded by the limited possibility for physical exercise.

Western fashion is not only often uncomfortable, but also downright debilitating and dangerous. The typical business suit of the 1920s, it is said, prevented proper ventilation of the body. Moreover, the collar and tie interfered with the free movement of the head, restricting neck and shoulder muscles, and giving rise to headaches and fibrositis. The nineteenth-century crinoline is an excellent example of the problems created by fashion. This stiff petticoat, which expanded the full dress skirt, was not only restrictive and cumbersome, but also risky. The diaphanous material frequently caught fire, and one woman in a crinoline was actually blown into the sea, where she drowned.

Oh, the suffering in the name of good taste.

CONCLUSION

The general microeconomic model normally assumes that individual utility functions are independent, that individual consumption functions are independent, and that tastes are exogenous. Such postulates are completely unrealistic for the clothing market, and thus the model, and its welfare implications, are not very useful for the consideration of fashion.

Fashion is a complicated phenomenon, influenced by many factors. This chapter has focused on one important cause of style changes in clothing: the competition for status. Status rivalry seems quite useful in explaining the *continual* changes in styles, especially in societies that permit upward social mobility.

For most people, what-to-wear is a mixed-motive game, involving elements of both cooperation and competition. The typical individual desires to clothe himself in the general manner of his contemporaries; he does not want to be considered odd. Within that prevailing style, however, he may want to be thought to dress extremely well, to be sartorially superior to the others. Veblen argues that his primary motivation is the desire to be considered highly placed on a socioeconomic hierarchy. The competitive use of clothing as an emblem of personal and class distinction is an important cause of changing dress styles, or fashion.

Mixed-motive games, or games with negative externalities, can often result in inefficient outcomes. In the case of fashion, it is possible that the entire society could be better off if the conspicuous consumption aspects of clothing and bodily adornment were eliminated. It is suggestive that utopians from Plato to Sir Thomas More to Mao Tse Tung dress all their citizens alike, generally in plain, undecorated, and durable cloth.

FOR DISCUSSION

1. Why do soldiers wear uniforms? Why do parochial school students? Girl scouts? Prisoners? Priests? What would be the costs and benefits to society if everyone were compelled to dress in virtually identical clothes?

2. Make a long list of goods and services and try to decide whether "fashion" exists in each item. Is there fashion in mothballs? ironing boards? steel? brooms? art? soap? books? stocks? Why is there fashion in some areas and not in others?

3. Which of the items on your list are primarily status goods? Does there seem to be any connection between status goods and fashion? Do you think that status items loom large or small in the U.S. economy? In the American Indian economy? In the People's Republic of China?

4. "The consumption of alcohol and tobacco, and some indulgence in fashionable dress . . . by workers are commonly classed as productive consumption, but strictly speaking it ought not to be" (Alfred Marshall, *Principles of Economics*, 1920). Comment. How

can one differentiate "productive" from "nonproductive" consumption?

5. Trinkets were among the principal items offered by Old World traders to the American Indians. Assuming free, uncoerced trade, where both parties to the transaction should benefit, did the exchange of corn, tobacco, or land for these tokens of bodily adornment help the Indian society even in the short run?

6. Do sellers cause or influence clothing fashion? How? Which ones? Were fabric manufacturers particularly happy about the mini-skirt?

7. Can rapidly changing fashion be considered "worse" in the clothing than in the automobile industry because of the lack of well-organized *used* clothing markets?

8. If Veblen is correct about the importance of conspicuous leisure in dress styles, why haven't clothes been even more cumbersome and confining? Surely the ingenuity of man could devise something more constricting than even the corset. Similarly, why aren't clothes even more sumptuous than they are? Does the theory of conspicuous leisure have something to say concerning this question?

9. What kinds of *empirical* studies might be done to help verify or refute some of the assertions and arguments in the article?

10. What is the effect of fashion on the clothing industry? How would the market structure, conduct, and performance be different if (a) there were no competitive consumption, or (b) the competition took the form of increasing sumptuousness rather than changing styles?

NOTES TO CHAPTER THREE

1. Thorstein Veblen, *The Theory of the Leisure Class* (New York: Mentor, 1953), p. 119.

2. Paul Nystrom, *The Economics of Fashion* (New York: Ronald Press, 1928), p. 9.

3. Edward Sapir, "Fashion," *Encyclopedia of Social Sciences* (New York: Macmillan, 1931), vol. 6, p. 140.

4. Dwight Robinson, "Economics of Fashion Demand," *Quarterly Journal of Economics* (August 1961)75:378-95.

5. John Maynard Keynes, "Economic Possibilities for Our Granchildren," *Essays in Persuasion* (New York: Harcourt, Brace, 1932), p. 365.

6. John Kenneth Galbraith, *The Affluent Society* (Boston: Houghton, Mifflin, 1969), pp. 138-54.

7. Veblen, *Theory of Leisure Class*, p. 42.

8. Ibid., p. 119.

9. Ibid., p. 120.

10. Ibid.

11. Quentin Bell, *Of Human Finery* (London: Hogarth Press, 1948), p. 24.

12. Veblen, *Theory of Leisure Class*, p. 49.

13. Ibid., p. 87.

14. Nystrom, *Economics of Fashion*, p. 9.

15. Bell, *Of Human Finery*, pp. 38–41.

16. J.C. Flugel, *The Psychology of Clothes* (London: Hogarth Press, 1930), p. 138.

17. William Hazlitt, quoted in Robinson, "Economics of Fashion Demand," p. 379.

18. Jane Dorner, *Fashion* (London: Octopus Books, 1974), p. 9.

19. Rene Konig, *The Restless Image: A Sociology of Fashion* (London: George Allen & Unwin, 1973), p. 140.

20. Dorner, *Fashion*, p. 13.

21. Herbert Blumer, "Fashion," *International Encyclopedia of Social Sciences* (New York: Macmillan, 1968), vol. 5, p. 344.

22. Sapir, "Fashion."

23. R. Broby-Johansen, *Body and Clothes: An Illustrated History of Costume* (London: Faber & Faber, 1966); Dorner, *Fashion*.

OTHER SOURCES

Paul Gregory. "An Economic Interpretation of Women's Fashions." *Southern Economic Journal* 14(July 1947), 148–61.

Paul Gregory. "Fashion and Monopolistic Competition," *Journal of Political Economy*. 56(February 1948), 69–75.

Charles King. "Fashion Adoption: A Rebuttal to the 'Trickle Down' Theory," in Stephen Greyser, ed. *Proceedings of the Winter Conference of the American Marketing Association*. (Chicago: American Marketing Association, 1963), 108–25.

George Simmel. "Fashion," *American Journal of Sociology*. 62(May 1957), 541–58.

Chapter 4

Social Forces

STORY I

Once there was a duchy called Irvana that lay in the fertile valleys of the Vagi Mountain. The people there were happy, friendly, and hard-working. They had great freedoms and a very reasonable living standard. They were a proud people, proud of their villages, their homes, and their work.

One fateful summer, a native son named Nicholai returned to the town. Nicholai had been the brightest young man of Irvana. He had left the duchy to gain further education and had become, for many years, a successful businessman in the outside world.

Nicholai came back to Irvana because he loved it. He remembered the beautiful white villages and green fields; most of all he remembered the people—proud, free, and happy. Yet upon his return, his heart filled with sadness. It was not that the duchy had changed much. It was, he felt, that it had not changed enough. The people were still strong and content, but they had not moved with the times. There had been a few improvements, certainly, but only a few. Irvana had not taken advantage of many new technological advances. Nicholai did not want his country to be backward or to be considered out-of-date.

Nicholai felt he could help Irvana. He saw how he could increase her output, using machines and modern techniques to replace hand labor. He would build his own modern factories as an example and a prod for Irvana to change her inefficient ways.

Not only was Nicholai a clever man, but he had also gained some

35

measure of wisdom. He had seen problems of advacement, problems of pollution and congestion. Never would he endanger his beloved green fields and pretty villages. He would not dirty the air or water, nor let his factories impose undue costs upon his neighbors. He would use his financial resources and his prestige and power to help Irvana grow materially, while eliminating the major costs of change.

But economic growth can affect society in countless ways. It can change men's attitudes, their outlook, their morality, and their contentment. All sorts of scenarios are possible, some good, some bad. Here, beginning with a happy people, we have cause to fear. Let us pick one possibility out of many, and spare Irvana much worse fates.

Nicholai built some factories. The problem with his jobs was that they did not satisfy the workers. Compared to other work in Irvana, this was dull, monotonous, routine. It did not demand men's minds, nor command their hearts.

Nicholai, at first, had trouble finding workers. Most craftsmen clung stubbornly to their outmoded ways. But he found some, enticed to boring jobs by higher wages. Those workers found themselves with higher income, higher wealth, higher consumption. Nicholai paid well and shared profits. His reputation for fairness and efficiency had not been overblown.

Now a touch of envy lurks in every heart. Men care about prestige and neighbors' attitudes and power. How smart a man is, or how strong, or how good, is relative to other men. There are few absolutes. In economic terms, worth is often based on what the market pays. And this creeps into the evaluation of the man himself.

The men who originally joined with Nicholai left their nice jobs for ugly ones. For them, the higher wages more than compensated. It brought increased wealth and living standards, both absolutely, and relative to their neighbors. They could buy things their neighbors could not, do things their neighbors could not. Their money, sad to say, could also buy political power and favors. Relative wealth was paramount here. But most important, the houses, clothes, and furniture of the factory workers were superior to others.' Their status rose, not only with consumption, but also with their wealth itself.

Part of the reason these men shifted jobs was to increase their status. Let us assume that without that change in relative position they could not have been persuaded to do the boring work of Nicholai's factories. The gain from the absolute increase in consumption would not have been enough.

To the extent these workers rose in status, others fell. Craftsmen could not purchase what factory workers could (though some tried). They could not enjoy the costly activities with their friends. The children wondered why other children had more. Could not they too?

So more workers switched to the boring but higher-paying jobs. And then some more. As more and more families opted for high income and consumption, it became harder still for those left behind. Each worker felt increasing pressure to work in the factories. Soon almost everyone worked there. Those left outside the factories were, indeed, outsiders.

The valleys of Irvana are still fertile, and the fields green. And the townsfolk, because of Nicholai, are richer in material goods. But workers dislike their jobs and there is less laughter and less happiness in the villages. All men cannot increase in status. Each man remembers the old days before Nicholai's factories, and each longs for the past. All wish they could return. All together. Individually, they cannot.

FOR DISCUSSION

1. Do you feel any pressure to be "successful"? What if you aren't?

2. Is it generally true that the more of one's friends who do something, the harder it is not to? If more and more friends "goof off," is it harder to study? If more and more acquaintances try pot, is it harder to abstain? As more and more families watch TV, is it harder not to? ("Did you see the Superbowl?"). Is it easier to do calisthenics alone or in a group?

3. How does Story I relate to a prisoner's dilemma game? Are there any similarities to what happened to Irvana and "neighborhood tipping," the marked transformation of neighborhoods from the predominance of one ethnic group to that of another?

4. Relate this story to Duesenberry's "demonstration effect." Why does the poverty line shift over time?

5. Is the competition for prestige at all comparable to the competition for military power? If Irvana didn't advance, wouldn't it just become bait for more prosperous and militaristic neighbors?

6. "If we begin with an ideal world, almost any change is likely to prove unfortunate." Discuss in relation to story I. Relate to the economist's use of the model of perfect competition.

7. Is tennis more fun to watch now that players are better? Is pro football, basketball, baseball more enjoyable for spectators than college equivalents? If participants spend more and more time and ex-

pense getting better vis-à-vis opponents, is this a move toward greater social welfare?

8. Isn't "progress" usually beneficial? When is it not? Are these just minor exceptions? What do you mean by beneficial?

9. Does the status of a job (other than its pay) matter in work selection? Do people choose optimal jobs? Is high mobility a good thing?

10. Why do you think teenagers drink and smoke so much? Purely for functional utility, or also for prestige, standing, and the need to conform? Is the amount of smoking optimal from an economic standpoint?

STORY II

"Five meters is not too tall," said Fred Johnson, and his nostrils flared in anger and determination. "My son is not going to be a runt."

Fred stood up, but his back remained bent. He began rubbing his spine. Martha, his companion, kept quiet, to allow his anger to pass.

They were alone in the waiting room.

Fred was over three meters tall. He was large for any age—except his own. He stood head and shoulders above his own father, who always stated his height in the ancient system of measurement. Fred's father was "six feet small." Both father and son wished they were taller.

"You don't know what it's like to be a man—and be too short," continued Fred. He paused for effect, but kept rubbing his back. He wished that he were home, under the massage machine. He would like to ask Martha to help him rub, but that would never do. He was mad, and he wanted to remain so. Anyway, Martha was busy fiddling with her knee supports.

"I'm too short," said Fred; "Now hush, Martha, you know that it's true." Martha had not batted an eye. She was steeling herself for the speech she knew was forthcoming. Her knees hurt, but she must maintain her composure. This was an important argument to win. Her son's future life was at stake.

"If I had only been taller I could have been somebody," continued Fred. He stopped his incessant self-massage for emphasis, and eyed his companion. "You know I could have.

"Tall people have all the advantages," complained Fred. This was his lifelong gripe. "Tall people are the best athletes. Christ, why shouldn't they be? Height's an advantage in everything. People look

up to tall people. (Martha started to smile, but checked herself.)
"They're respected. They get the best of everything. They get the
best jobs, they get the pick of the girls—"
"Fred!" Martha interrupted sharply. Fred blanched.

Martha stood up. She had sat still too long, and her back was
throbbing. Fred immediately straightened up, as he always did when
he and Martha were standing. It was fortunate that the waiting room
ceiling was high. Though Fred was not a tall man, he frequently
bumped his head in old buildings.

Martha bent over, in part to ease the strain on her aching back, but
more in order to remain at a lower altitude than her companion.
Then she lowered her voice and spoke strongly but quietly. She knew
that Fred blamed all his failings on his stature. He had never forgiven
his parents for making him below average. But she had to convince
him.

"Why did we go to a height advisor," she asked, "if we weren't
going to take her advice?" The height advising business, begun
immediately after the genetic breakthrough that had allowed height
selection, had mushroomed in the past decades, a mushrooming
closely paralleling the rapid increase in average height, an increase
termed the height inflation. Martha had always felt that there was
an insidious connection between the advisors and the inflation. It
was Fred who had insisted that they see an advisor, and so they had.

But the advisor, instead of advocating increased size, had warned
against the drawbacks of excess absolute size, while minimizing the
importance of being relatively tall.

"We should never have gotten a woman advisor," snarled Fred.
"What do women know about height?" Martha hunched over a bit
further. She always wished that, for Fred's sake, she were smaller
than he.

"She came highly recommended," reminded Martha. "The
Asworths used her, and the Walkers." She paused. "We could have
always gotten a second opinion. We might still get one. Perhaps they
will let us postpone this appointment. We could come back tomor-
row, or ——"

"Nonsense!" cut in Fred, "We are here, and the time has almost
come. We know something about the statistics and the trends, and I,
at least, know what it's like to be too short. My son is not going to
go through what I went through, what I go through. He is not! He
is not! He will be five meters, and he will be tall!"

Fred was practically yelling. Martha closed her eyes, tightly. She
was trying to calm her tremors. Her knees ached, her back throbbed.

Worse still, she felt dizzy and lightheaded. She wasn't sure she was thinking clearly. She hoped it was just her blood pressure medication. Damn that medication. That was another problem about being too tall. . . .

She sat down; Fred sat beside her. He seemed contrite. She knew that he was sorry he had raised his voice. She put her hand on his knee and started rubbing. Fred closed his eyes.

"I just want our son to have every advantage," he murmured.

"So do I," she said softly. "So do I."

Martha thought of her son-to-be. This was to be the only child they could have. They had been a little unlucky in the drawings. But she was by no means bitter. While some families might have as many as six children, others were not even permitted a single offspring. This was to allow some diversity in family size, while checking the overflowing world population. She had been thankful when her time had come, and she had not emerged empty-handed. And a boy! It was what they would have chosen. Now she secretly wished it had been a girl. Fred would not have been so inflexible about a girl's height. He still believed—as did many—that the woman should be shorter than the man. There were't any good reasons for this belief, except that was the way it always had been. And since many people wanted it this way, it was the way things had generally remained.

"Fred," she said. "Really. Think of the physical problems. Knees, back, ankles, heart. We weren't built to be so tall."

"We weren't built to walk upright either," snapped Fred, "yet it hasn't hurt us much." Fred was sitting down. He paused. "Look, I know there are problems, now." Fred emphasized the "now." "But science will solve these problems. It just takes a little time. There's a lot of money going into height research. Soon we'll just have one little operation at birth that will correct everything." Fred had stood up, bent over, and was rubbing his back. "Even the really tall won't need those awful spinal operations every year. One little operation will correct everything."

"You don't know that," cried Martha. "You may be dooming our son to a life of agony, just to be tall." She continued. "And think of the social problems caused by the height inflation. The old buildings have to be converted or torn down. The old furniture is no good. Nothing old is much good now," she said. "And the height inflation has all the problems of the old population explosion, and you're the one who always said that we should——"

She was interrupted by the opening of the waiting room door. A man entered. A large man. Another patient. Fred immediately straightened up, stood tall, and looked the man in the neck.

The man seemed friendly, introduced himself as Jim, and then asked, "You here for a spinal operation too?"

Fred shook his head.

"No, of course not," said Jim, looking down at Fred. Fred was too short to require that operation. "Of course not." And Jim sneered.

The sneer did it. Shortly thereafter, when the doctor came in, Martha signed for five meters.

The next day Fred met Jim at the prearranged location. Fred was smiling.

"Thanks," he said, as he handed Jim a packet of money. "You were great. It worked perfectly. My kid's gonna be tall!"

"But I was worried," he continued, "you were almost too late."

"Sorry," replied Jim. "I think I must have passed out for a bit on the way over. You know. The blood pressure medication."

FOR DISCUSSION

1. Relate to story I. Relate to options.

2. How tall would you like to be? Does it depend on how tall everyone else is? Would you like to be below average in height? Above average? Can more than a majority of people be above the median height? What do you think would happen to average size if people could choose their children's height? What would be the effects if couples could choose the sex of their children?

3. What would correct government policy be in story II? What should it be currently, given that individuals can choose how many children they have?

SOCIAL FORCES

Man is a social animal. He lives in a society of other men and naturally is influenced by them. His attitudes are influenced by the attitudes of that society, his perceptions are affected by the perceptions of others. Similarly, his economic choices and decisions are, to a large extent, molded and shaped by social values and social pressures.

All men have a few basic physical needs, such as oxygen, water, food, warmth, etc. That these needs can be very cheaply provided is demonstrated by the fact that incredibly poor people, beginning with the cave man, have been able to survive. Over and above these necessities, man typically has a choice about what desires to attempt to satisfy; and he must also decide the manner in which to satisfy them. Society exerts a major influence over all such decisions.

When dining with others, for example, Western man must normally eat his meals with specific utensils—knives, forks, spoons—on a plate or in a bowl; liquids are to be drunk from cup or glass. And there are a myriad of other customs to be observed. Man's wearing apparel is similarly specified. The Western male must usually wear shoes, socks, pants, even underwear; particular shirts, trousers, coats and ties are required for formal occasions. It is generally not necessary for government to enforce such prescriptions. Each individual's desire to conform, to be included rather than excluded, is normally sufficient.

This clustering of action (and attitude) is called *custom*. For any individual, the existence of custom brings both benefit and cost. Custom decreases the range of socially acceptable choice, while making the actions of individuals in society more predictable and more coordinated. Two points deserve special emphasis here. First, custom clearly influences man's social behavior, including his economic behavior. Second, there is no automatic mechanism, no invisible hand as it were, to insure the correct amount of custom or to insure that the location of the clusters will be optimal from some social criteria.

Economists do not usually discuss customs or focus on social influences. The man in the economic model is a rational fellow who follows his own self-interest and has a single measure called *utility* that he attempts to maximize. Moreover, it is generally assumed that his preference function is not directly affected by the consumption path, work pattern, or general life-style of others. Preferences are data, exogenous variables, uninfluenced by economic outcomes.

This heroic assumption can lead to fruitful insights, but it seems to assume away much that is interesting in the real world, and can result in misleading and incorrect conclusions. This chapter argues that preferences are largely interdependent, and mentions some normative implications of introducing some consumption externalities into the general microeconomic model.

If a man's preferences depend, in part, on the economic actions of others, what is the exact nature of that relationship? There are a large number of plausible assumptions that might yield worthwhile hypotheses. Here we argue that a person cares about his relative position in society. For example, if an individual finds his relative income or wealth declining, ceteris paribus, his utility decreases. This kind of interrelationship has been examined by such economists as Veblen, Duesenberry, and Galbraith. For one thing, man is concerned about his status in society, and this is a relative rather than an absolute concept. A man's economic status or prestige depends heavily on his relative income and relative consumption levels. Even a man's sense of personal worth is affected by the relative values the economic system places on his contribution.

In order to uphold his position in society, a man must meet certain forms; he is expected to behave in certain prescribed ways. To the extent that his social standing depends upon his economic position, he will be expected to consume at a certain level. The kind of house he lives in, the car he drives, and the parties he gives should reflect his position. A business executive cannot skimp on the liquor he serves his guests, or the car in which he chauffeurs his clients or peers, or even the clothes he wears in their presence. In order to maintain his status, his position, his job, he is often forced into a certain life style. And his required consumption expenditures will increase as society grows richer.

Relative consumption also matters for reasons of direct functional utility. The value of certain goods and services (vacations, plays, dinners, etc.) may be enhanced by consuming them with friends and neighbors. If a man's relative income falls, he may find it increasingly difficult to accompany higher-income friends desirous of consuming higher quality and more expensive items. As contemporaries increase housing expenditures, the individual may find it impossible even to live in the same neighborhood.

A man's economic status affects whom he meets, whom he marries, where he lives. It affects his opportunities. A person, even one not particularly gratified by economic power or satisfied by material possessions or enthralled by conspicuous consumption, may rightly care about his place in the economic hierarchy.

If one's ranking matters, one's relative as well as one's absolute position, then there are externalities, and decentralized decision making may well lead to suboptimal results. If, for example, it is relative consumption that gives prestige, then ceteris paribus, total consumption expenditures will be too large. If it is private rather than public goods that buy status, our mix of purchases, as Galbraith has argued, may overemphasize personal possessions. If our income, rather than our leisure or the kind of work we do, promotes respect, then we may tend to work too hard, and at the wrong kinds of jobs.

CONCLUSION

Man is a social animal and is dramatically affected by his social environment. His preferences are influenced by the economic actions of others. Advertising is but a minor source of such influence.

There are many ways that another's actions may affect an individual's preferences. One interesting and plausible way is that, for a variety of reasons, man cares about his *relative* wealth, income, and consumption.

Some important normative implications derive from this assumption. The most crucial is that, even assuming perfect competition, economic "progress" may lead to inferior equilibriums. Story I illustrates how social forces may cause worker alienation.

In story II, man cares about his *relative* height. This story emphasizes how growth (in a literal sense!) may prove inimical to society. The main point of both stories is that social forces create externalities, and where important externalities exist, decentralized and competitive actions may lead to undesirable results.

FOR DISCUSSION

1. "Conventional welfare analysis stands and falls with the theory of the immutable isolated consumer. If wants can be influenced, what do we mean by the satisfaction of wants?"[1] Comment. Who should decide what wants to satisfy? Since man is a social animal, with preferences molded by the environment, does this really mean that all of conventional economic welfare analysis is uninteresting and/or misleading?

2. "The more truth there is in this relative income hypothesis—and one can hardly deny the increasing emphasis on status and income-position in the affluent society—the more futile as a means of increasing social welfare is the official policy of economic growth."[2] Comment. Aren't we better off, happier, than our great-grandparents? Don't we have better food, housing, sanitation, medication, etc.? Do you think that the importance of status and income position increases as the society grows richer?

3. "It is thus not so much the utility of cash earnings which provides the initial incentive to men to make them start clearing large areas of bush and plant cash crops, but rather a desire on the part of a few enterprising men to prove themselves as entrepreneurs and ultimately to accumulate more assets and thereby either confirm or establish their position as 'big men.'"[3] Comment. What are the implications of this for government policy designed to promote progress? What are the implications for human welfare?

4. Does what brings status (wealth, power, strength, intelligence) differ among different societies? If so, what accounts for this difference? Does the economic system influence what kinds of things bring prestige and respect? Does economic progress?

5. Think of another way social forces affect preferences other than through prestige and status desires. What are some of the economic implications of this effect?

6. Given that social pressures do affect preferences, what are the implications, if any, for public policy?

7. Are there customs and clusters that you find less than ideal? Are the current calendar, the English language, the customary system of measurement, the typewriter keyboard, and the location of cities optimal? How do you feel about wearing neckties or high heels, going to cocktail parties, and tipping cab drivers? Can or should anything be done about such customs?

NOTES TO CHAPTER FOUR

1. Stanislaw Wellisz, "Discussion on the Doctrine of Consumer Sovereignty," *American Economic Review* 52(May 1962):287.
2. E.J. Mishan, *The Costs of Economic Growth* (Staples, 1967), p. 120.
3. Scarlett Epstein, "Innovation of Cash Crops in New Guinea Subsistence Economies," reprinted in H.W. Arndt, "Prestige Economics," *The Economic Record* 48(December 1972):585.

OTHER SOURCES

H.W. Arndt. "Prestige Economics." *Economic Record* 48 (December 1972).
"The Doctrine of Consumers' Sovereignty." *American Economic Review* 62 (May 1962). Papers and comments by T. Scitovsky, J. Rothenberg, A. Berson, S. Wellisz, W. Baumol.
Erich Fromm. *The Sane Society.* New York: Holt, Rinehart & Winston, 1955, chapter 5.
John Kenneth Galbraith. *The Affluent Society.* Boston: Houghton, Mifflin, 1969, chapter 11.
John Kenneth Galbraith. "Economics as a System of Belief," in *Economics, Peace, and Laughter.* Boston: Houghton, Mifflin, 1971.
Sidney, Hook, ed. *Human Values and Economic Policy.* New York: N.Y.U. Press, 1967.
Edward Miller. "Status Goods and Luxury Taxes." *American Journal of Economics and Sociology* 34 (April 1975).
Thomas C. Schelling. "On the Ecology of Micromotives." *Public Interest* 25 (Fall 1971).
E.F. Schumacher. *Small is Beautiful.* New York: Harper & Row, 1973.
Thorstein Veblen. *The Theory of the Leisure Class.* New York: Mentor, 1953.
Walter Weisskopf. *Alienation and Economics.* New York: Dell, 1971.
Morris Zelditch, Jr. "Social Status," *International Encyclopedia of Social Science.* New York: Macmillan, 1968.

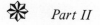 *Part II*

Exchange and Pricing

INTRODUCTION

At the heart of microeconomics lies price theory. Economists have rightly emphasized the importance of prices in a market economy, the crucial information they relay to prospective buyers and sellers, and the role they play in rationing society's scarce resources. It might be argued that there has been a tendency among economists to focus too much on price, and too little on other variables, such as product quality and design. Yet there are topics concerning pricing and prices that have received scant economic attention. This section discusses five such areas, all related to exchange and the way prices are set.

Chapter five examines gift giving, where price equals zero, and discusses the role of gift exchange in primitive and modern society. The next four chapters deal more directly with pricing and pricing methods: haggling, scalping, tipping, and the cover charge. The general procedure is to explain where such phenomena are likely to occur, and to describe some of their principal economic effects.

✳ *Chapter 5*

Gifts

Gift giving and receiving form an important component of our social life. We receive gifts from birth, when we are showered with presents, until death, when well-wishers provide the bereaved with flowers or other tokens of concern and affection. Virtually all the important social events of our lives are marked by the receipt of cards or gifts: weddings, birthdays, anniversaries, graduations, bar mitzvahs. Even a house purchase may bring housewarming presents. The giving and receiving of cards and gifts accompany many of our general holidays, such as Mother's Day, Valentine's Day, Easter. Much of the magic of Christmas is intimately connected with the making, buying, wrapping, giving, and opening of presents. Gifts may also be given for no apparent reason, occasion, or event, but simply as surprise tokens of love.

Many goods given gratis might be considered as gifts, such as treating for drinks or having friends for dinner. Many services are also provided free of charge and could conceivably be categorized as gifts. Much of our social exchange, of favors, respect, ideas, even recipes, have elements of gift giving. The focus here is upon the material present, often identifiable by its special wrappings. The emphasis is not upon the normal social exchange of favors, nor upon the various forms of charity, from the giving of alms to the poor to the donation of blood to the Red Cross.

Gift giving, even a reciprocal exchange of gifts, stands in sharp contrast to exchange by barter. Barter requires the relinquishing of one good in order to secure another. In gift exchange, on the other hand, the giving up is voluntary. While there are often strong social pressures to return gifts, there are no legal sanctions against noncompliance, for no binding contract has been entered into. In barter, both parties determine what will be exchanged, and haggling is permissable. In gift exchange, it is the giver who unilaterally selects the exact good that changes hands, though there may be hints, customary rules, or other pressures that affect his choice.

The gift-giver has more discretionary power over what good, if any, to relinquish, but he has less real freedom to withdraw from a continuous process of exchange. While the pressures to engage in specific market or barter exchanges are generally small, there is usually a strong social obligation to accept an offered gift. The acceptance of a gift helps create or affirm a cordial relationship. To refuse a gift usually engenders ill will. The acceptance of a gift produces further pressure to reciprocate in some manner. It is therefore entirely possible for an individual to become trapped in a system he had no desire to enter into. Even refusal to return something as innocuous as the Christmas card greeting can have undesirable social ramifications.

It is the social aspects of gift giving that most differentiate it from market transactions. Among other things, gifts can serve to express affection, to promote fellowship and solidarity, and to reaffirm social worth. Such social effects are largely absent in market transactions, in which parties to the exchange are playing economic rather than social roles.

While gift giving is primarily a social event, it does have important economic consequences. Gift giving influences the kind of goods demanded, as well as the timing of purchase, and possibly even the household's consumption/saving choice. One dramatic illustration of the impact of gift giving on business is the effect of Christmas on retail sales. In December sales of apparel stores in the United States jump some 80 percent over normal months; sales in general merchandise stores rise almost 90 percent. Overall December retail sales are consistently more than 20 percent above the normal monthly average.[1]

This chapter is divided into three parts. In the first, a major implication of microeconomic theory regarding gifts is examined. Unfortunately, because of the social nature of gift giving, classical economic theory is not terribly useful for understanding the role of gifts in society. The second part describes the importance of gift exchange in a number of tribal societies. Viewing gift giving from different cultural perspectives can help to illuminate some important aspects of gift exchange in modern society. The final portion discusses the qualities of those specific types of goods that are often purchased as gifts. These are but a few of the wide variety of issues concerning gift giving that are deserving of attention.

GIFTS AND MICROECONOMIC THEORY

Economists have largely ignored the phenomenon of gift giving. The general economic approach, however, is that man is a rational being and will therefore try to give that amount and those particular presents which will maximize his own utility. And perhaps the principal implication from micro theory regarding gifts is that, except for strictly monetary presents, the custom is economically inefficient. The argument parallels the well-known analysis of the inefficiency of government food-stamp programs and housing subsidies. Such programs are inefficient because direct income subsidies that cost the government no more than the specific product subsidies can provide greater utility to the recipients. If they wish, the recipients can spend th whole of their extra income on housing or food. If they spend only a part on these products, economists presume they prefer the expenditure pattern they selected for themselves. Similarly with gifts. A gift of $10 should provide at least as much material benefit as the gift of a $10 necktie.

The conclusion that money gifts are always more efficient than material presents requires some very strong assumptions. One assumption is that the recipient's consumption pattern does not affect the giver's utility. A related and more crucial postulate is that the act of caring and giving, of bestowing the proper present, doesn't directly affect the recipient's utility: he would be at least equally content had he just enough additional income to have purchased the good for himself. This postulate is generally incorrect, since it ignores the essential social nature of gift giving. In the real world, since individuals do not have complete knowledge, they often desire the signals and symbols of affection and esteem that gifts can provide.

There are other assumptions implicit in the conclusion that gift giving is inefficient. One postulate is that an individual's preferences are always best known to himself, and that he can act rationally with respect to them. This may not be the case if there are problems of personal temptation, or if there is an unwillingness to buy oneself desired commodities because they seem too "frivolous." A further assumption is that the transaction costs of market exchange are negligible. Again there are exceptions in the real world. On a trip I might see something unusual and inexpensive that a good friend might like. Buying it for a gift could prove more efficient than any available market arrangement. I know he would have trouble purchasing it for himself. Contacting him immediately has costs. There may be problems with my buying it on the hopeful assumption that he will repurchase it from me. Formal or informal contractual agreements making me his purchasing agent can run into difficulties. While market transactions are usually more economical than gift exchange, if explicit contracts are costly to make or enforce, then reciprocal gift giving may prove more efficient than market exchange. This may be a usual circumstance for many primitive societies.

GIFT GIVING IN PRIMITIVE SOCIETY

Nineteenth-century German economist Bruno Hildebrand's three-stage theory of economic development emphasizes the importance of the medium of exchange. The first stage is represented by a natural or barter economy, which is gradually supplanted by money exchange, and finally by credit. Studies of tribal society belie this simple schema. Gift giving is often an older and vastly more important form of exchange than is barter in primitive economies, and thus should be placed at an earlier stage. Moreover, a fundamental ingredient in many gift-giving arrangements is the supposedly advanced notion of credit. As Marcel Mauss perceived, gifts generally require countergifts, and often time must elapse before presents can be returned.[2] A posthaste gift return is often considered improper, for it implies a refusal to stay indebted. In the words of a French maxim, "Excessive eagerness to discharge an obligation is a form of ingratitude."[3] Similarly, an exact-return payment may be considered an affront, suggesting a desire to transform a social into a more business-like relationship.[4] Gift exchange thus frequently entails an implicit, albeit unusual, form of credit, where the original recipient remains under some obligation until the gift is repaid. While there are no formal contractual arrangements, some countergift is often dictated if honor and reputation are to be preserved.

The Kula[5]

Gifts accompany virtually every ceremony in Melanesia and are also provided for a wide variety of privileges and services. Gifts are given to the garden magician, to village mourners at funerals, to unmarried girls for sexual favors, etc. The Melanesian vocabulary contains an enormous number of words specifying particular categories of presents.

The *kula* stands at the apex of this Melanesian gift-exchange system. It is public and ceremonial, rooted in myth, backed by traditional law and surrounded by magic. Yet in its essence, the kula is simply a passing from hand to hand, between designated partners, of prestigious but generally useless objects. The exchange of kula items takes place in a circular fashion around the islands. Necklaces are passed clockwise from island to island, and armshells counter-clockwise. These kula objects have little practical value other than for decoration, and even here they are often too valuable or cumbersome to be worn. But first-class necklaces and armshells are more than mere valuables. Each has a name, a personality, a past, and perhaps even a legend attached to it. To possess one is considered exhilarating yet comforting. Their owners may handle and gaze at them for hours. Moreover, while they are never kept for any length of time, temporary possession provides the owner with prestige and perhaps renown. The kula valuables form a favorite subject of tribal conversation, gossip, and gloating.

Kula exchange is usually reserved for village chiefs, who have a number of lifelong kula partners in other tribes. Their cermonial exchange of necklaces and armshells often requires large overseas expeditions; herein lies the great economic significance of the kula. The expeditions facilitate large amounts of exchange among the islands, in the form of gift giving and barter. The kula thus promotes both economic trade and political friendship, creating a vast network of relationships among potentially rival tribes.

A relationship similar to the kula often exists between common tribesmen in neighboring maritime and agricultural villages. Vegetables and fish are exchanged by specific partners in ceremonial and reciprocal gift giving. This exchange, known as *wasi*, promotes economically beneficial division of labor among the islanders.

The natives also engage in barter, but sharply distinguish this from kula, wasi, and all other forms of gift giving. Barter, or *gimwali*, is generally held in low esteem by the Melanesians. Gimwali lacks the social aspects of gift exchange. There is no ceremony, magic, or special partnership. When asked about certain transactions, whether they belong to one class or another, a native is apt to say in a deprecating tone: "That was only gimwali." It is significant that villagers will barter, but not exchange gifts, with members of tribes that are usually treated with contempt.

Gimwali can be done with strangers, and in a free manner. Gift giving, on the other hand, requires social intercourse and often an elaborate form and manner of presentation unnecessary in barter exchange. When criticizing indecorous or hasty procedure during kula, a native may say: "He conducts his kula as if it were gimwali."

While sharp bargaining occurs in gimwali, direct haggling is never permitted in gift exchange, for it would demean the entire process. In gift giving, however, there is sometimes implicit negotiation to help insure that both parties are happy with a reciprocal exchange. Even in kula, since village chiefs have a number of partners in other tribes, "bait" may be used to indicate publicly interest in, or bid for, a partner's newly acquired armband or necklace. Second-grade treasure, such as pigs or axe blades, are often given to solicit specific kula valuables.

In kula, wasi, and many other types of gift giving, return presents are socially obligatory. It is sometimes impossible to return equivalent gifts immediately, and often it is bad form to attempt to do so. The requirement of delayed reciprocity helps create an obligation and trust relationship that unites villagers and tribes. Trust is more important in reciprocal gift giving than in barter or legal credit, since there is no direct means of redress should return gifts appear niggardly. While there is sometimes dissatisfaction with particular gift exchanges, most natives try to return a good equivalent. Social pressures are powerful among the islanders, especially in gift giving, since generosity is a principal virtue and meanness the most despised vice. Moreover, a reputation for fairness and generosity is useful in attracting a more munificent stream of presents.

The Potlatch[6]

Gift exchange also plays a pivotal role in the life of Indians inhabiting America's Northwest coast. Social ranking seems almost an obsession for these natives, and position is constantly challenged or reaffirmed at complex ceremonies known as *potlaches*. The great potlatches are winter festivals which last for weeks. They are marked by the lavish distribution of gifts by the host and sometimes by the actual destruction of valuables in a competitive show of wealth.

Potlatches are often given at critical life events: birth, adoption, puberty, marriage, death. There are also face-saving, totem-pole, and vengeance potlatches. For some tribes, the house-building potlatch is the largest and most important type. Visitors from other villages remain for a considerable part of the winter and help construct a dwelling. There is much ceremony and festivity, culminating in the presentation of valuables to the numerous guests.

At a major potlatch the host is aided by his *numaym*, which is principally a paternal descendant group. Past gifts of blankets and other valuables by the host to his numaym obligate them to repay, on demand, at phenomenal rates of interest. These repayments provide the host with enough property to distribute among outside guests to bring honor to his name, and to his numaym.

The goods distributed at the potlatch consist almost entirely of treasure items of little practical value. They are not intended to satisfy the comfort wants of the guests, but first and foremost the status demands of the host. The social ranking of the host, or of his progeny, largely depends on the relative size of his potlatch. Social standing resides not in the accumulation of wealth, but in its public disposition. Potlatch gifts are thus different from payments for work done. Instead they may be considered as prestige investments, goods bestowed on guests in their capacity as potlatch witnesses.

The potlatch is the principal method among the Indians by which relative rankings are not only established, but also validated. While the host is judged by the size of his potlatch, guests are ranked by the relative value of the gifts they receive. The inequality of the gifts reflects the host's judgment of relative social worth.

While general gift exchange is common among the natives and usually associated with fellowship and good spirit, the potlatch is sometimes used for economic warfare. A perceived slight or insult by one close in status but from a different numaym may be met by a potlatch challenge—to see who can give away or, more often, destroy the most valuables. Failure to match one's rival is tantamount to defeat. This is the motivation for the spectacular vengeance potlatches used to ruin an opponent. The spectators are the ultimate judges in these ostentatious displays of conspicuous destruction.

The vengeance potlatch—vast destruction of property to destroy a rival—is the monster-child of gift exchange. The usual potlatch, however, is a time of ceremony and festivity, often accompanying a major social event. It is sometimes the occasion for joint constructive work, as the building of houses or totem poles. And in aboriginal times it may have served as an important method of income distribution. Before contact with white traders, the natives were more numerous and less prosperous. It is believed that gifts then given during potlatch contained more utilitarian items that helped alleviate short-run misfortunes. The aboriginal potlatch, as well as serving prestige functions, may also have been a form of disaster insurance, distributing essential food and wealth between neighboring numayms.

Gift exchange is vastly more important in these primitive societies than in the modern economy. Yet gift giving in developed countries remains a significant phenomenon, with somewhat similar motives and effects. For example, gifts can build friendships and goodwill; they often help solidify kinship relationships. At weddings they are one aspect of the creation of linkages between the uniting families.[7] Ostentatious gift giving can be used to preserve rank and increase prestige. A debutante's coming-out party, for instance, can be perceived as primarily an investment in status.[8] And our exchange of gifts at Christmas can be likened to a gigantic, friendly potlatch, involving millions of families and with many budgets ending in fundamental imbalance.[9]

GIFT GOODS

It has been estimated that perhaps 10 percent of all retail sales in the United States are related to gift giving.[10] Goods received as gifts are somewhat different from commodities that would be purchased for oneself, and it is not possible (nor perhaps desirable) for individuals to compensate completely for this fact. In other words, gifts do influence the type and kinds of goods purchased and produced in our economy.

The social aspects of gift exchange are of utmost importance. The content of a present is generally subordinate to its significance as a token of the social relationship. Moreover, the manner of giving is often as important as what one gives. Virtually anything can be given and welcomed as a present if it is given in the right spirit. Nevertheless, certain types of goods are more presentable and acceptable as gifts than others.

Flowers are an appropriate gift for almost all occasions, as, to a somewhat lesser extent, are candies. Flowers are beautiful and fragrant; there is the implication that these are beautiful things to brighten the lives of beautiful people. As Emerson wrote in his curious essay on gifts: "We love flattery even though we are not deceived by it, because it shows that we are of importance enough to be courted. Something like that pleasure, the flowers give us: what am I to whom these sweet hints are addressed?"[11] The rationale for candies follows the similar logic of sweets for the sweet.

Gift giving is a sign of social relationship, and what we give may be considered a signal of how we view the recipient. Thus the appropriateness of flowers, candies, etc. Conversely, it is often fitting to give something representative of oneself. Thus Emerson argues that a poet should bring his poem, the miner a gem, and the shepherd his lamb.[12] An extreme instance of self-presentation through gifts is the display of masculinity on the part of a new father in the giving of cigars.[13]

While it is the thought that counts, the relative value of the gift also matters. It matters since the gift is a presentation of oneself, an indication of one's generosity, and a signal of one's affection. The value of the good may be reckoned by the time spent by the giver in making the present, or in selecting the most appropriate item, or it may be determined by the price. There are, of course, limits of good taste on the maximum price since there is often a social obligation to repay gifts, and because it is considered vulgar to try to buy friend-ship or affection. These are items whose value is destroyed if bought or sold in the marketplace.

Because affection becomes tainted by marketplace values, it is cus-tomary to tear off price tags before giving store-bought presents. Similarly it is the mean person who precisely computes the price of goods received. Nonetheless, the conspicuousness of gifts, and the signal attached, requires that they usually be generous. A Chinese proverb says: "In ordinary life you must be economical; when you invite guests you must be lavish in hospitality."[14] A dinner guest not only receives ample portions, but is given better than the usual fare.

Gift goods are generally near the top of the line. They are often brand-name items, with well-known trademarks for superior quality. One gives an expensive Parker pen as a graduation present, not a collection of Bic pens. Manufacturers cater to the need for known prestige goods for gift purposes. Lancer ads show hosts quickly recognizing and appreciating their guests' gift of this particular wine. Hallmark creates the card "for those who care enough to send the very best." Gift giving generally rewards the high-quality product-dif-ferentiation advantages of the well-known established firm.

Presents are usually luxuries. Gift shops are packed with nonessen-tials, with frills and knickknacks. It is often in bad taste to give some-thing too useful to a poor friend or relative, for it smacks of charity. It may tend to rob the gift of its sentimental value and humiliate the recipient with the implication that he is being treated as a needy per-son rather than as an intimate.[15] As Emerson writes: "We wish to be self-sustained. We do not quite forgive a giver. The hand that feeds us is in some danger of being bitten. We can receive anything from love, for that is a way of receiving it from ourselves; but not from any one who assumes to bestow."[16]

The suitability of any particular gift depends on the occasion and the relationship of the parties concerned. The closer the relationship, the wider the latitude of choice of gifts (and usually the more appro-priate the present). Many items are too personal or too expensive to be given by mere friends or acquaintances. Some presents require intimate knowledge of one's tastes, decor, sense of humor, etc. The more distant the relationship, the more important the implicit rules of gift giving, the more likely are gifts to be luxury items of well-known high quality.

CONCLUSIONS

Social exchange, the exchange of courtesies, pleasantries, ideas, and favors, is pervasive. Gift giving is an aspect of social exchange involving material goods. In savage society, gift giving is also often the dominant method of economic exchange. Even in our advanced society, the exchange of gifts has important effects on our economic and social lives.

It is the social ramifications of gift giving that sharply differentiate it from market exchange. In primitive societies, gifts play a total social role, encompassing aspects of the religious, magical, economic, judicial, and moral.[17] Among the Melanesians, gift giving is "one of the main instruments of social organization, of the power of the chief, of the bonds of kinship, and of the relationship in law."[18] In all societies, gift exchange is a powerful force helping to bind social groups together.

Gifts also bring various recipients and donors into comparison. This is demonstrated in most dramatic fashion by the potlatch ceremonies, whose principal function is to create and preserve social-status rankings. But comparisons created by gift giving are present in all societies. Modern parents, for example, try to give equivalent presents to their children to emphasize their equal love for them all. Conversely, to avoid the invidious comparison of whether mother or father cares more, it is a general practice for parents to give gifts jointly.

The role gifts play in status comparisons is enchanced by the high visibility of much gift exchange. Large ceremonial gatherings are integral components of the potlatch and kula exchanges. In modern society, gift exchange is also somewhat conspicuous. Presents usually are opened before some kind of audience, often including the donor. Indeed, one reason gifts are wrapped is to provide an element of mystery and surprise and to allow the giver to witness the recipient's initial reaction. General conversaion, especially around Christmas, is often directed to the exact nature of presents given and received. This conspicuousness of gift giving influences the type of goods exchanged. In both primitive and modern society we find that gift goods are comprised largely of luxury items of well-known high quality.

Economists have generally ignored gift exchange. Present economic theory has little of interest to say about it. Yet its economic and social importance in both savage and modern society makes it an ideal topic for further research and study by all types of social scientists.

FOR DISCUSSION

1. "Never borrow money from a friend (or do business with him)." What is the basis for this adage?

2. Does the marketplace decrease the value of certain services? Which ones? Why is there a tendency to look down on paid companions, gigolos, and prostitutes?

3. What are the pros and cons of a society where gift giving is the principal method of exchange?

4. "In spite of the success of a business society in increasing productivity and in providing for human wants, it has a tendency to undermine itself because of its inability to generate affection. It is a positive-sum game in which everybody benefits, but in which the game itself is apparently so lacking in emotional effect that it does not produce loyalty, love, and self-sacrifice. Very few people have ever died for a Federal Reserve Bank" (Kenneth Boulding, *Beyond Economics* [Ann Arbor Paperback, 1970], p. 235). Do you agree? Aren't many businessmen quite protective toward their corporations? Aren't there any social ramifications of pure economic exchange?

5. Relate gift exchange to the business practice of reciprocity.

6. What is the relationship between gift exchange and geographic mobility?

7. Do you think the McDonald's gift certificate will prove highly profitable? Why or why not? How about one for Dunkin' Donuts? For Saks Fifth Avenue? For Tiffany's? Why give a gift certificate instead of money?

8. Why is there a Mother's Day? Which groups had an incentive to create one?

9. What are the principal economic effects of Christmas?

NOTES TO CHAPTER FIVE

1. U.S. Department of Commerce, *Survey of Current Business:* Business Statistics, 1973 edition, pp. 59-60.

2. Marcel Mauss, *The Gift* (New York: W.W. Norton, 1967), pp. 1-45.

3. François La Rochefoucauld, *The Maxims* (London: Oxford University Press, 1940), p. 73.

4. Barry Schwartz, "The Social Psychology of the Gift," *American Journal of Sociology* (July 1967)73:6.

5. Most of the material in this section on kula exchange comes from Bronislaw Malinowski, *Argonauts of the Western Pacific* (New York: Dutton, 1950). Secondary sources include: Paul Bohannan, *Social Anthropology* (New York: Holt, Rinehart & Winston, 1963), pp. 229-39; Cyril Belshaw, *Traditional Exchange and Modern Markets* (Englewood Cliffs, N.J.: Prentice-Hall, 1965), pp. 12-52; Mauss, *The Gift* pp. 18-31.

6. A great deal has been written about potlatch, some of it contradictory. Material in this section comes from a variety of sources, principally: F.H. Boas, *Kwakiutl Ethnography* (Chicago: University of Chicago Press, 1966); Helen Codere, *Fighting with Property* (Gluckstadt, Germany: J.J. Augustine, 1950); George Peter Murdock, *Rank and Property among the Haida*, Yale Publications in Anthropology #13 (New Haven: Yale University Press, 1936); H.G. Barnett, "The Nature of Potlatch," *American Anthropologist*, (July 1938)40:349-57; Ronald P. Rohner and Evelyn Rohner, *The Kwakiutl* (New York: Holt Rinehart & Winston, 1970), pp. 95-105. Stuart Piddocke, "The Potlatch System of the Southern Kwakiutl: A New Perspective," *Southwestern Journal of Anthropology* (Autumn 1965)21:244-64; Bohannan, *Social Anthropology*, pp. 253-65; Belshaw, *Traditional Exchange*, pp. 20-29; Mauss, *The Gift*, pp. 31-37.

7. Belshaw, *Traditional Exchange*, p. 50.

8. Bohannan, *Social Anthropology*, p. 259.

9. Claude Levi-Strauss, *The Elementary Structure of Kinship* (Boston: Beacon Press, 1969), p. 57.

10. Belshaw, *Traditional Exchange*, p. 50.

11. Ralph Waldo Emerson, *Essays*, Second Series, (Boston: Houghton-Mifflin, 1865), p. 154.

12. Ibid., p. 155.

13. Schwartz, "Social Psychology of the Gift," pp. 1-11.

14. Alpha C. Chiang, "Religion, Proverbs and Economic Mentality," *American Journal of Economics and Sociology* (April 1961), 20:258.

15. Peter M. Blau, *Exchange and Power in Social Life* (New York: Wiley, 1967), p. 111.

16. Emererson, *Essays*, p. 156.

17. Mauss, *The Gift*, p. 1.

18. Malinowski, *Argonauts*, p. 167.

19. Levi-Strauss, *Elementary Structure of Kinship*, p. 59.

Chapter 6

Haggling[a]

A remarkable feature of contemporary economic life is that market exchange can transpire very naturally without verbal exchange. A final consumer may simply take an item from the shelf, some money from his pocket, change and receipt from the clerk, and leave the store. If words accompany the purchase, they may refer to the weather or to whom a check should be made out. Sometimes the qualities of the product are discussed. Talk may involve mention of price, but this is normally only by way of idle chatter over its level, or inflation, or to inform the buyer when the tag is missing. Haggling is the exception rather than the rule in most consumer goods markets.

Most final goods in the United States are sold at standard terms and standard prices. This is also the case for many intermediate goods. The terms are offered on a "take-it-or-leave it" basis, with "give-and-take" effectively precluded. Economists, except when discussing labor markets, usually assume the existence of this standard form of contract "negotiation."

There is no haggling, nor any reason for it, in the world of perfect competition, where decision-makers face horizontal demand-and-supply curves. Nor will haggling occur if only one of the participants has market power and already knows the reservation price of the other. But haggling is possible where the reservation price is not known, or where both parties possess some degree of market power (and there is something to bargain about). Looking at real world mar-

[a]Coauthored by Fred Gramlich

kets, this seems to suggest that haggling is possible virtually everywhere.

In a simple scenario of price determination, either buyer or seller announces a price. In this chapter we assume it is the seller, which appears to be the more usual situation; the analysis is symmetrical in either case. If the buyer dislikes the seller's initial figure, he may make a counteroffer. If this bid induces the seller to modify his announced price, haggling has occurred. In other words, it takes two to haggle. The communication required for haggling need not be oral, though it generally is, and it can involve the quality of the item or the terms of the contract, as well as, or instead of, the price.

FACTORS AFFECTING HAGGLING

Personal Preferences
Some people enjoy haggling; they relish the opportunity to outwit an opponent. They love the reputation for shrewdness they may gain from haggling. On the other hand, many people are poor bargainers. Others may regard it as an intrusion of self-interest upon goodwill. One does not usually haggle with family or friends because this asserts the narrow individual interest over the social relationship. Those who wish to make a conspicuous display of their wealth may also wish to refrain from a bargaining process which may indicate something of a penny-pinching mentality. Finally, the rich and/or powerful may dislike haggling with the poor because of the unattractive distributional implications.

Emotion and Dependence
The dynamics of haggling can generate emotion and sometimes unpleasantness or bad feeling. A buyer desperately wishing not to antagonize the seller may avoid the risk by not quibbling. Most consumers will not bargain over the price of a new alternator for their car at a gas station in unfamiliar territory late at night. Nor is it usually wise to haggle with a doctor over the price of an urgent operation for actue appendicitis. The patient is too dependent upon the outcome of the operation, and haggling may affect that outcome.

The Value of Time
Bargaining takes time, and time is an important economic resource. Rich buyers, particularly those with a high earned income, are likely to value their time highly and not waste it bickering over the price of exchange. Those with lower time costs—housewives, the unemployed, the retired—are more likely to bargain. The wealthy, on the other

hand, are more likely to purchase the time of others to represent them in potential price negotiations.

The value of time varies over time. A buyer may not haggle if time is short: he has a plane to catch, he is late for an appointment, he is eager to get into a performance but needs a scalped ticket, etc. The value of time also varies for institutional sellers. Stores with busy periods will have a policy not to bargain. Not only does it waste the employee's time, it wastes the time of everyone in the queue at the counter, and this affects the attractiveness of the store. Since it takes at least one person to man a shop, small stores with occasional business are more likely to be receptive to bargaining.

The Value of Goods in Exchange

If the purchase is of small value, there is little potential gain from haggling. Thus, there is little haggling over low-price retail items—a newspaper, chewing gum, a cup of coffee—since the potential gain to either buyer or seller is incommensurate with the added time costs.

Conversely, the large buyer may find it pays to haggle about terms, quality, and price. This may also lead to better deals in subsequent purchases. The seller finds the threat to change suppliers unless concessions are forthcoming more menacing if made by a large buyer. Since purchases are generally larger for producer than consumer goods, these are often the markets where haggling occurs.

Institutional Control

There are strong reasons to expect haggling to be less prevalent in retail markets where stores are large. Haggling creates problems for the coordination and control of the large organization. Revenue projections are more difficult, tax calculations more arduous, employee theft more likely. A customer thus finds he cannot haggle with the salesperson, for the clerk is not allowed to bargain. He must follow orders.

In order to haggle, decision-makers must be involved. Those doing the bargaining must have some power or incentive to set the ultimate price. The owner/salesman in a small store has this power and may have the incentive. The clerk in a large chain does not. Indeed, one way a seller can attempt to discourage haggling is by making communication with decision-makers difficult.

Subsequent Dealings

Haggling can affect the buyer's or seller's reputation, influencing other transactions. A retail seller's reputation for allowing haggling may attract an unappealing mix of customers. Bargain hunters with time to burn may flock to the seller, while the rich avoid him.

A low-price outcome in one transaction may strengthen the next purchaser's bargaining position. Sellers are thus more receptive to haggling when transactions are secret, or the exchange is part of a close-out sale. In general sellers are more prone to haggle about unique rather than standardized goods. With unique items, such as secondhand goods, haggling is less likely to lead to disgruntled customers because postpurchase comparisons are more difficult; the seller's future negotiation position is also less jeopardized. One reason large buyers can gain price concessions is that they are in some sense unique. The seller can agree to grant such concessions to others—if they purchase as much.

Price Discrimination and Oligopolistic Coordination

Sellers may promote haggling as a useful method of price discrimination. For Italians selling leather goods in the open markets of Florence, haggling allows them to distinguish between the ill-informed tourist and the sharp-eyed connoisseur. Similarly, used-car and furniture dealers in the United States can increase their profit if they are able to employ haggling to help determine demand elasticities.

Haggling makes price coordination more difficult, however. Oligopolists may therefore attempt to ban haggling and other forms of price concessions. If they desire to promote price discrimination, it will be through other, less destabilizing methods.

MARKETS FOR HAGGLING

Housing and Labor

Two important areas where haggling often occurs in the United States are in housing and labor markets. A house is generally the major consumer durable purchased by a family. A used house is unique and usually sold by another family, whose business is not selling houses. The large number of sellers and the expensive and unique nature of the product, combined with the immediate availability of decision-makers, imply that haggling might be a common feature of this market, which is indeed the case. A principal exception is the builder of many similar, geographically clustered homes, who might wisely refuse to haggle with any single prospective buyer.

For rentals, there is generally less haggling where the renter is an individual family, interested in an apartment in a large complex of similar units. On the other hand, where rental space is unique (a room in someone's home), or the renter is special (a drawing card at a shopping center), or the renting organization is willing to occupy a significant percentage of the space available, negotiation is more likely.

When a laborer works full time for a corporation, it is generally, though not always, the corporation that sets price around which haggling may or may not occur. An individual laborer without unique skills may be unable to bargain successfully about the offered conditions of employment. On the other hand, one with rare talents —a twenty-game winner, an outstanding executive—may have the power to haggle or to actually set his own price. When labor is organized, workers have the power to bargain about wages set by management. Indeed, United States law requires "good faith bargaining" —haggling—in such situations.

IS HAGGLING GOOD OR BAD?

In a certain sense haggling is wasteful; it takes time, can generate adverse emotions, and may disrupt planning. Exchange at some arbitrarily determined level between the reservation prices of the participants might be more efficient. But such a solution is generally neither practicable nor desirable for both parties. Each has an incentive to understate his true willingness to deal, and either or both may believe a better personal outcome can be achieved through haggling.

Haggling often causes price discrimination, which can have both beneficial and detrimental efficiency effects. Price discrimination of intermediate goods can allow inefficient firms in the consuming industry to survive while efficient ones are failing. On the other hand, discrimination in final goods markets usually has the effect of increasing the output of monopolized industries, thereby increasing allocative efficiency.

Since information is often gained and exchanged during haggling, especially concerning particular buyer needs regarding deliveries, payment terms, etc., such negotiation can improve economic efficiency. Consider a situation where each seller has his own standard contract form. If market information of buyers is incomplete, or if there are costs of changing suppliers, even a relatively competitive market may diverge from efficiency. Without haggling, sellers may not have sufficient incentive to offer those special terms that particular buyers would find most advantageous. This situation is not unlike the case where prices exceed the competitive level solely because information limitations remove the advantages to price reductions. Where haggling increases information, it may also increase social welfare.

The distributional effects of haggling are not clear-cut. Rich buyers with large time costs may have less tolerance for haggling, and thus be willing to pay higher prices. Conversely, the rich may have achieved their financial position in part by being good bargainers. The rich are also more likely to purchase expert negotiators to bargain for them. In addition, the rich buyer or large firm is more likely to buy in large quantities, and is more able to extract pecuniary price concessions through haggling.

The welfare effects on third parties are also mixed. The presence of haggling makes collusive arrangements among oligopolists harder to maintain. But it may also make it more difficult for potential entrants to obtain accurate price information; thus, entry becomes riskier and less likely. And for consumers, the absence of precise price information makes comparison shopping, and rational buying, more difficult.

Whether or not others haggle affects the expectations and actions of buyers and sellers. For example, because most people haggle over new cars, list prices tend to be set well above average price. This forces all potential buyers either to haggle or to be discriminated against. Conversely, if no one bargains about typewriter prices, it is difficult for any individual purchaser to make much headway. This stability of either haggling or standard pricing arrangements may prove harmful or beneficial to any particular individual, depending on his situation and proclivities.

POLICY

The government requires haggling in labor markets when management confronts a union. The good-faith bargaining rule is used as a way of assuring that management deals with the elected, collective representative of the employees, rather than with the workers individually. It is not haggling per se that is valued, but enforced management recognition of the union's legitimacy.

Government also sets prices in certain markets, thereby precluding haggling over rates. But in general, the United States government has taken a largely laissez-faire attitude toward bargaining. Where haggling occurs, usually no one has forced the two to tangle. But because haggling requires at least some market power, one of the participants might prefer standard terms and prices to haggling.

Haggling can affect efficiency and equity. Its third-party influences are varied, but real. Yet ideal government policy toward haggling is probably noninterventionist. The potential benefit from government action is not likely to be large, while the monitoring and enforcement costs are probably prohibitive.

CONCLUSION

Haggling is a pervasive economic phenomenon, though somewhat less prevalent in developed countries where time costs are high. The large established sellers found in advanced nations also tend to eschew haggling because it make planning and control (and collusion) more difficult.

Market structure characteristics affect the likelihood of haggling. Haggling may be most common when bargaining power is somewhat equally distributed, as in the case of bilateral monopoly. In retail markets, haggling occurs most often when sellers, like buyers, are small. Haggling arises normally in many intermediate goods markets because purchasers, like sellers, are often large. When power is disparate, the stronger party has the power to impose, and may prefer, take-it-or-leave-it conditions. There are, of course, exceptions to this rule, as when a large seller finds it advantageous to price discriminate via haggling.

Theoretically, the economic effects of haggling are many and varied. However, the dearth of economic evidence regarding haggling makes it difficult to assess its real world importance. But given the likely costs and problems of any attempted government regulation, we can surmise that the current laissez-faire policy is probably a wise one.

FOR DISCUSSION

1. Do you expect to find haggling about airplane tickets? doctor fees? Christmas trees? used books? banquet speaker salaries? Explain. Might it matter who the buyer is? An individual or a large corporation?

2. "The market for television advertising time is elaborately organized. While networks have posted rate cards, negotiated agreements are the rule on *major* sales. An advertiser can get a better deal if he risks waiting to buy until a week or two before show time" (Richard E. Caves and Marc J. Roberts, *Regulating the Product* [Cambridge, Mass: Ballinger, 1975], p. 104). Comment. Might you have predicted this situation?

3. What factors determine whether buyer or seller normally sets the price? Does it matter who does?

4. Should the federal government be willing to haggle about its employees' wages? Should it negotiate or haggle about its purchases of paper clips? Of roads? Of spaceships?

5. Is haggling more a cultural or economic phenomenon? Knowing just economic information, but little about the social aspects of the nation, could you predict the amount of haggling, and where it is likely to occur?

6. "Never look a gift horse in the mouth." Relate to gifts. Relate to haggling.

7. If other consumers haggle in a particular market, does this affect whether or not you will? Why?

8. How would you go about gathering data and doing empirical research regarding haggling?

 *Chapter 7*

The Cover Charge

There is a wide variety of pricing strategies and arrangements in the real world, including sales, specials, loss leaders, discounts, haggling, bundling, tying, and minimums. The pricing arrangement discussed in this essay is what nightclubs call the "cover charge" and economists deal with under the heading of the "two-part tariff." Here, the term *cover charge* is used to describe the fixed price that allows access to certain goods or services, usually for a particular period, following which the consumption of the commodity is generally variable among users. Thus, the ticket price for a basketball game is not considered a cover charge, but the fee for entering an amusement park is.

THE BUYER'S PERSPECTIVE

Consider the simplest case. There is a cover charge, but no additional cost to the customer. The potential purchaser is attempting to compare this scheme with one where there is no cover, but a variable charge depending directly on consumption. This choice is nicely illustrated by the American tourist's decision of whether or not to buy a Eurail Pass.

The Eurail Pass provides unlimited train travel in Europe for a limited amount of time. The question to be considered is whether it is a worthwhile purchase. We will assume there is only one other alternative: traveling by train at the normal fare.

Before the fact (ex ante), if the traveler knows that he is definitely going to spend more on rail travel than the cost of the pass, he should purchase the pass. However, even if he is planning to spend less on rail travel at regular prices, he may still want to buy the pass, given some elastacity in his demand. Neglecting various complications, owning a Eurail Pass makes additional out-of-pocket expenses for train travel equal to zero. This can lead to additional travel, and greater utility.

Figure 7-1 gives an individual's demand curve DD for rail travel. Let us ignore income effects, or assume the income elasticity is zero, so that DD is a constant utility demand curve. With normal fare OB the customer will purchase OD amount of train service, and gain consumer's surplus given by triangle ABC. It is clear that if the Eurail Pass costs less than rectangle OBCD, it should be purchased. But once the individual owns a pass, the additional price for extra travel in the period equals zero, and OE of train travel will be consumed, providing additional benefit of triangle CDE. Thus, the pass should be purchased as long as its cost does not exceed quadrangle OBCE. In other words, an individual initially planning to spend only $80 on rail travel at normal prices may nonetheless find a Eurail Pass costing $100 to be wise purchase.

On the other hand, the after the fact (ex post) knowledge that the amount traveled OE would have cost more at normal prices (rectangle OBFE) than did the purchase of the Eurail Pass does not confirm that buying the pass was a good decision. The price of the pass can be less than rectangle OBFE, while still greater than quadrangle OBCE. In other words, receiving $120 worth of rail service for a $100 Eurail Pass does not prove the purchase was a wise one.

Other real-world examples of a cover charge with no variable out-of-pocket expenses might include "all-you-can-eat" dinners, entry-fee

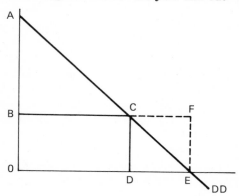

Figure 7-1.

free-ride amusement parks, WATS telephone service, or membership in American Express, health clubs, or the Automobile Association of America. Prepaid health plans may also be included in this category.

THE SELLER'S PERSPECTIVE

Consider a monopolist selling a single product, with no fear of entry. For simplicity, assume a constant marginal cost, OA in figure 7-2. Theory tells us that if the firm cannot price discriminate, it maximizes profits by selling that amount where marginal revenue equals marginal cost, charging price OB.

Now let the firm impose a cover charge. This option can increase the company's profits. Let us examine the simplest case, where all customers are identical, with demand curves DD. Again we assume that income effects are negligible. In this case, by pricing at marginal cost, and with a cover charge equal to triangle ACF, the firm can truly maximize its profits. Total revenues for the firm are the summation of rectangles AOFG (unit sales) plus the sum of all triangles ACF (cover charge). The firm produces that amount where (unit) price equals marginal cost.

The cover charge may be considered a form of price discrimination, a special brand of volume discount. Each customer is sold the first item at OA plus the cover, while each successive purchase costs only OA. Were there a fixed cost associated with selling to each customer equal to the cover, this pricing arrangement would be "cost justified."

If customers do not have identical demand curves, the seller maximizes profits by setting unit price equal to marginal cost, but charging a different cover for each buyer, just sufficient to exhaust his consumer's surplus. This has the same net effect as perfect price discrimination, and like all discrimination, requires some ability to prevent

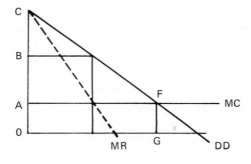

Figure 7-2.

resale of the commodity. It is also similar to perfect price discrimination, or any pricing scheme that appropriates the entire consumer's surplus, in that the solution can be a bit precarious. Increasing the cover charge to any buyer by as much as a penny eliminates all sales to that customer.

THE SOCIAL PERSPECTIVE

Classical microeconomic theory holds that, with no externalities, the optimal amount of production for each industry occurs where demand equals marginal cost. Should price be set above marginal cost in only one industry (e.g., mass transit), individuals will use too little of that service. A consumer deciding whether to use his own car or public transport for an additional trip will be comparing the marginal cost of additional car miles to the price (greater than marginal cost) of additional transit miles and, from the social perspective, will too often use his own vehicle.

For a company with decreasing costs, a single price per unit set equal to marginal cost will leave revenue less than total cost. Subsidies are then necessary for the firm to survive. But most government subsidies conflict with the efficiency and/or equity goals of society. The two-part tariff has been discussed by economists as a solution to this problem. Like straightforward price discrimination, it has been suggested as a way for the regulated natural monopolist to provide the optimal amount of output while avoiding the problems of subsidization. In the real world, regulated telephone services and electricity and water supplies are often priced to include a flat fee, with additional charges related to the amount of consumption.

The allocation of resources will be efficient with a two-part tariff if unit price is set at marginal cost and the cover charge does not cause any potential customer to eliminate all his purchases. If the cover charge does cause some buyers to leave the market, the two-part tariff will not result in the best allocation of resources. For the case of a uniform cover, the second-best solution may require a lower cover charge to keep more buyers in the market, and a unit price that diverges from marginal cost.

Providing the consumer with an option of either a fixed fee or a unit charge (the Eurail Pass) also affects economic efficiency. This alternative will usually increase consumption, but not necessarily by the right people. The Eurail Pass owners buy too much from the viewpoint of society, consuming as long as their demand is positive, even though their marginal benefits are less than the marginal cost of production. And those not opting for the flat rate will purchase the correct amount only if unit price is set equal to marginal cost.

CONCLUSION

The cover charge is an interesting pricing arrangement that can often increase profits. It is employed in a variety of situations. One is when sellers find exclusion of nonpayers feasible and desirable. Tennis clubs and amusement parks provide examples. Fixed charges can be used to cover common costs, as those large fixed costs of telephone companies, electrical utilities, and other natural monopolies. And flat fees are sometimes supplied to reduce consumer uncertainty and to spur efficiency in production. This is part of the logic behind prepaid health plans and the single charge for complete orthodontic work. These are just some of the areas where the cover charge is found in the real world.

The term *cover charge* is not very precise. An admission to the circus or the movies is probably not a cover charge. On the other hand, the initial fee for stepping into a taxi or a fixed price for local telephone service probably is. But how about rentals of cars, bikes, buffers or parking spaces, where the price varies with time rather than actual use? And how about the plumber who demands some fixed amount for any time worked between zero and one hour?

Whether such practices are or are not considered cover charges is not crucial. What does matter is that such real-world pricing schemes be analyzed and understood.

FOR DISCUSSION

1. If you were president of Tiffany's, would you charge people simply for walking in the store? What would be the effect if you did?

2. Is a ski lift pass a cover charge? What is the effect of this pricing arrangement? Why aren't ski lifts priced per ride rather than per day? Is a subway fare system that allows complete travel between all points for a single price a cover charge? Why aren't passengers charged per length of the ride (as they are in the Bay Area Rapid Transit)?

3. "Some nightclubs have too much business on weekends, so they add a cover charge applicable only to these crowded periods. Such action encourages customers to come in during less busy periods of the nightclub's operation" (Douglas North and Roger Leroy Miller, *Abortion, Baseball & Weed* [New York: Harper & Row, 1973],

p. 133). Comment. Why not raise liquor prices and have a minimum? During busy periods why may restaurants have a minimum, but usually not a cover? Why don't they set a time limit on how long clients can remain at a table?

4. Contrast overtime wages and cover charges.

5. To get access to Dun & Bradstreet company financial information, there is a fixed fee as well as a unit price. Why do you think D & B set prices in this manner? Might they have any problems preventing the resale or distribution of their information?

6. Can a perfect competitor impose a two-part tariff? Why or why not?

7. What should be public policy toward the cover charge? Should a patent-based monopoly be permitted to impose a two-part tariff?

SOURCES

Martin Feldstein, "Equity and Efficiency in Public Sector Pricing: The Optimal Two-Part Tariff." *Quarterly Journal of Economics* 86(May 1972):175–87.

André Gabor. "A Note on Block Tariffs." *Review of Economic Studies* 23(1955):32–41.

Richard and Peggy Musgrave. *Public Finance in Theory and Practice.* New York: McGraw Hill, 1973, p. 681.

Yew-Kwang Ng, and Mendel Weisser. "Optimal Pricing with a Budget Constraint—The Case of the Two-Part Tariff." *Review of Economic Studies* 41(July 1974):337–45.

Walter Oi. "A Disneyland Dilemma: Two-Part Tariffs for a Mickey Mouse Monopoly." *Quarterly Journal of Economics* 85(February 1971):77–96.

Roger Sherman. "Club Subscriptions for Public Transport Passengers." *Journal of Transport Economics and Policy* 1(September 1967):237–42.

✳   *Chapter 8*

Tipping

A tip may be described as a gift, usually a small amount of
money, given voluntarily for a service rendered. It should
be noted that the gift is small, not entirely compulsory,
and is given after the service has been performed.

WHO IS TIPPED?

Tipping is partly determined by custom, and thus varies from country
to country. In Spain, for example, theater ushers are tipped, a practice not prevalent in the United States. On the other hand, in Finland
barbers are never tipped, and it might be considered an insult if a tip
were offered, for the tip can imply a distinctive class or hierarchical
position between the parties. The Finn may reasonably believe the
offer demeans both himself and his job. For even where the practice
is widespread, a tip may denote a lack of status. Amy Vanderbilt[1]
and Emily Post,[2] for example, advise that room waiters are tipped
but never hotel managers, skycaps but never reservation clerks,
stewards but never a ship's officer. It is perhaps significant that
"boys" and "girls" jobs are often tipped: delivery boys, shoeshine
boys, hatcheck girls, etc.

Tips are thus given for some services in the United States, but
clearly not for all. The service generally has to be menial and physical (porter, bellhop) rather than more skilled or higher status (doctor,
lawyer, accountant). The service is usually personal (barber, caddy,
waitress, masseuse). Thus, cab drivers are tipped, but not bus drivers.
Ball park attendants may be tipped if they perform a special service

such as cleaning your seat. The same is true for strolling restaurant musicians, if they play your request. On the other hand, personal services not personally paid for, or performed by fellow workers, are definitely not tipped (trainers, makeup men, secretaries).

Finally, face-to-face contact is generally important. Home delivery newspaper boys are tipped if they collect personally, not if the bill is sent by mail. Mailmen, milkmen, garbagemen, an answering service may all provide more or less personal service, but are not tipped. Sometimes, however, a Christmas "bonus" is given. For nurses, housemothers, and even secretaries who provide face-to-face con- tinuous intermediate-status service, a "gift" is often appropriate. There is something less demeaning in these lump-sum bonuses or gifts, Thus, expensive high-fashion hair stylists in big cities now expect Christmas bonuses rather than weekly tips.[3]

Jobs requiring tipping are often those a servant might perform: personal, menial, low-status services requiring face-to-face contact. While this describes most instances when tipping is in order, there seem to be a number of occupations, especially borderline ones, where custom makes the determination. For example, ship stewards are tipped, but not airline stewardesses. And it is not entirely clear whether moving men should be tipped. Repairmen, however, gen- erally aren't, nor are sales personnel.

CUSTOMARY NATURE OF TIPPING

Perhaps the most outstanding feature of current tipping is its cus- tomary nature. Social conventions largely tell us not only whom to tip, but how much. Tipping is often virtually obligatory, and in- deed, the tip has been incorporated as a compulsory service charge in many European restaurants. The worker is no longer clearly inferior to the consumer. Convention creates an implicit, though vague, con- tract among near-equals.

For the worker, the custom of tipping might to some extent be viewed as the service equivalent to piece-rate pay. Rather than the contracted objective criteria of the employer, however, the service worker has to depend on the whims and generosity of the con- sumer, a special problem with nonrepeat customers. A convention- alization of tips thus benefits the worker, stabilizing the expected return for service, making income slightly more predictable, and enabling a wiser choice of occupations. At the same time, of course, extra service could be rewarded with an extra large tip.

With respect to tips, the customer to a large extent now simply wants to do "what is right," what is expected. That is why he reads

Amy and Emily. He tries to tip whom it is customary to tip, the customary amount, in the customary manner. If service is adequate, he generally wants no unfulfilled expectations, no hurt feelings. He may not want to be overly generous, or appear vulgar, but he may especially not want to cheat anyone or appear cheap. And if he is "risk averse," he may especially not want to grossly undertip anyone and have that person create a scene. Given a variety of national customs, this could be a partial reason why tourists generally tip heavily. There are, of course, other reasons for large tips: to be known as a big tipper, to reward excellent service, etc.

One of the real drawbacks to tipping is the problem it creates for fair-minded people. They are required to learn the correct amount and procedures for tipping—and sometimes they err. Tipping also creates minor problems for rational initial purchase decisions, since two prices (one quoted, one conventional) must be discovered in order to learn the full cost of purchase.

WHY TIPPING?

Popular belief holds that *tip* derives from eighteenth-century English usage and stands for the words "to insure promptness,"[4] but tipping was known as far back as the roman era and is probably much older. The word *tip* itself may come from stipend, a bastardized version of the Latin *stips*, meaning gift.

The tip begins as an incentive and reward for good service. It allows the buyer to withhold partial payment until the quality of the service is observed. This is more helpful the less sure he is of the reliability of the worker. The demeaning nature of the tip partly derives from this point: there is an implication that the worker is perhaps untrustworthy, or lacks good workmanship habits or high ethical standards. In part, too, the tip may be demeaning in what it is the buyer who unilaterally determines the amount of the tip, the worth of the act. (There may also be an aura of charity for the poor, but working, man.) A contract specifying the various graduations of service quality and their price would clearly be less demeaning. Given the small nature of the service, however, and the small amount of the tip, the "transactions costs" are generally too far out of line to make this a feasible alternative.

For the employer of the worker (for those workers not self-employed) the tip performs a similar function. The employer's product is probably tied to the worker's services, as dinners are with waitress services, room accommodations with bellhop services, ship travel with steward services, etc. The employer wants reasonable service to be provided, but may be unable to immediately supervise the worker. The customer is best able to judge the adequacy of a simple personal service, and the custom of tipping provides an immediate positive monetary incentive to the worker; complaints provide a negative incentive. Total remuneration is thus, hopefully, more closely allied with service quality than if a flat rate were paid. Again, though, there may be an implicit distrust of the worker, especially compared to the trust given to the customer.

It is not surprising that tipping has often been attacked for its "undemocratic" and demeaning nature. The institution, however, remains strong. As Emily Post writes. "Tipping is undoubtedly an undesirable and undignified system, but it happens to be in force."[5] Her advice is, of course, to tip. Tipping seems to be a custom that individual action cannot readily eliminate. Collective action, however, has sometimes been effective. In the airline industry, tipping of stewardesses was never permitted; which of course is easier than stopping an established custom. And supposedly Communist countries have met with some success in eradicating tipping.[6]

It is not at all clear, though, that the elimination of tipping would be socially desirable. Tipping can perform a useful function, and the main social drawback, its demeaning nature, can easily be overstated. The question is largely one of attitude. It is doubtful, for example, that the current tipping of barbers, waiters and waitresses, or cab drivers dramatically decreases either their dignity or social prestige. These people are now tipped principally because it is expected, because it is the custom.

More Effects of Tipping

Tipping can be an important component of workers' pay. For example, it is estimated that more than 60 percent of the total earnings of the more than 250,000 waiters and waitresses employed in large establishments come from tips.[7] On the other hand, only 2 percent of chambermaids' earnings derive from this source.[8] When compared to a straight wage, pay that includes tips will be more variable. To the extent that there is risk aversion, workers should demand a slightly higher average wage than otherwise. This is also the case if the job is indeed demeaning. A countervailing factor is the greater ease of income-tax evasion with tips, thus increasing effective take-home pay.

Where there is tipping, the base wage (employee) or the basic service cost (self-employed) should be less than in its absence. In the case of a waitress, since a large part of her income comes directly from the consumer, the restaurant can give her less. One effect of tipping, then, where the worker is an employee, is that when business declines, she is less of a burden or fixed cost. Her income, however, fluctuates greatly. Where there is tipping one might therefore predict fewer "firings" and more "quittings" than without the custom.

Looked at another way, the income of the worker depends on the base wage, the generosity of the customers, and the success of the enterprise. The more standardized the tip, the more important becomes enterprise success. We have here a crude form of profit (actually sales) sharing. This is carried the farthest in European restaurants where the service charge is automatically added to the bill. Perhaps this is a minor reason why hawking is more common there than here.

It is illuminating to contrast the tip with the sales commission. In the latter, income depends on making immediate sales, the understanding being that walk-in customers generally must be "sold," or non-walk-in customers found. Tipping usually occurs when it is fairly certain that walk-ins will buy or have already bought (restaurants, hotels, ships, taxis). The function of the tip is to help ensure adequate service. The emphasis may be more on future sales. Both the tip and the commission are forms of sales sharing (though the commission is contracted and paid by the firm), and thus both decrease "overhead costs."

From the employer's perspective, tipping may be beneficial; it reduces supervision costs and direct wage expenses. The desirability of tipping is also affected by state and federal laws. Social Security regulations, for example, exempt the employer from adding his contribution to income earned from tips.[9] On the other hand, some states do not include tipped income when determining whether minimum wage requirements have been met.[10] An interesting economic effect of tipping is that it causes price discrimination against the softhearted, the big tipper. If bigger tips are directly related to inelasticity of demand, tipping could prove one minor method by which firms could increase their profits.

It is important to distinguish areas where services are likely to be repeated (barber) and those where they are not (taxi). In the former, past performance and the expectation of future contact helps generate a fairly stable system of acceptable pay for acceptable service, though there may be some continuing "jockeying for position." And while each separate "unwritten contract" between barber and customer may well be different, a constant small tipper, ceteris paribus, can generally expect less service compared to the big tipper.

With nonrepeat games the situation is less stable. A worker may well vary service depending on how he sizes up the customer—on what he believes is the customer's tip-service schedule—and on the cost of different levels of performance. In nonrepeat games, the worker has much less information and is more likely to categorize incorrectly. The same is true with the first encounter of a repeat game, though the worker, with similar information, may well select a different level if he expects repeat purchases. For a customer where misclassification is likely and may create problems, some sort of signal is in order. For example, since women are notoriously small tippers,[11] one desiring excellent service (and willing to pay) might try to differentiate herself, perhaps by paying part of the tip in advance. Similarly, smart male dressers are expected to tip more.[12] They had better be prepared to tip more, Emily advises, or face unfulfilled expectations.

In nonrepeat games, the customer is most on the honor system to tip adequately. (The worker, though, still has the threat of expressing disapproval or creating a scene.) The conventional nature of the tip, and its small size, protects not only the worker but also the transient customer, who is less likely to be distrusted and more likely to receive adequate service. The conventional rules themselves, necessarily simple and easily understood, may create minor problems. For example, if a restaurant tip is expected to be 15 percent of the bill, a small purchaser may have to distinguish himself if he is to receive service equal to those ordering an expensive meal.

Overall, the custom of tipping probably has had only the most minor effect on the total price of most purchases. If business is steady and the tip standardized, the tip becomes similar to a small surcharge. If tipping conventions are less rigid, and workers are risk averse, the total price of purchase may be marginally higher with tipping. More important, the less rigid the conventions, the more the potential for price discrimination.

Tipping probably noticeably affects the full price of a service or commodity only in the case of some small purchases. This is because tiny tips are not socially acceptable. Thus, for a forty-cent taxi ride, Amy advises, do not expect change back from a dollar.[13] If leaving less than a dime or quarter is implicitly banned, low-price-high-volume businesses may find the custom of tipping unduly raising their full prices. Hence it may make sound economic sense for a Dunkin' Donuts or a Chock Full o'Nuts restaurant chain to place conspicuous "Tipping Prohibited" signs throughout their franchises.

CONCLUSION

Those occupations where tipping is prevalent are usually low paying, or else the small amount of money involved would have no allure.

The service performed is often personal and simple: the tipper alone benefits, is best able to judge the worth of the service, and can do so immediately. The task is often menial, and there may be an implicit superior-inferior status relationship in the act. Face-to-face meeting helps to facilitate payment.

The custom of tipping tends to make pay more proportional to service actually rendered. Since a straight wage for variable work is not unusual, however, with tipping there is the possible implication that the worker may be a bit untrustworthy, or at least needs immediate tangible reward to work effectively. For many tipped jobs today, any such conclusion is probably unwarranted.

Some occupations receive tips largely because it is the custom. Other occupations that might well be tipped are not. It is doubtful, for example, whether any startling changes would result if tips were eliminated for waiters, barbers, and cab drivers or begun for ushers, stewardesses, and gas station attendants. Perhaps even more interesting is speculation on whether we might like to withhold partial payment until service is complete, and then somewhat unilaterally determine the worth of services performed by plumbers, garage mechanics, TV repairmen, doctors, mailmen, actors, salesmen, etc. At least one of the many problems is that as tips increase in size, the greater is the incentive for the customer to "cheat," and the larger is the price discrimination against those who don't. This is undoubtedly one reason why, from the point of view of the customer, tips are never a large part of total cost.

Overall the effects of tipping are varied, but probably fairly minor. The principal function of the tip is as an incentive and reward for good service. And though much tipping is largely obligatory and conventionalized, an extra-large tip can be given for extra or exceptional service, a small tip for poor service. The obligatory nature of tipping permits this "punishment" for bad performance. Perhaps the greatest drawbacks of tipping are its potentially demeaning nature, the search problem it causes well-intentioned travelers, the occasional nuisance of tipping, of needing the right change, and the difficulties that can arise if implicit rules of tipping are not clear or are not followed.

FOR DISCUSSION

1. A recent British survey concerning tipping concludes that "it tends to decrease management control, increase recruitment problems, and irritate and embarrass many customers" (*Why Tipping?* Economic Development Committee, National Economic Development Office, Millbank Tower, London, 1972). If most people dislike tip-

ping, why does it continue to exist? Why won't individual action simply put an end to it?

2. If others tip, does this affect the likelihood that you will tip? Why? How do you determine how much and whom to tip?

3. Why would Communist countries try to abolish tipping? Is this easy to do? Is tipping likely to spring up again? Why or why not?

4. What would be the principal effects if tipping were abolished for barbers in the United States? For waitresses?

5. Do you expect there to be more tipping in a developed or a less developed country? Why? Do you expect tipping *rates* to be higher in New York City or in Muncie, Indiana? Explain.

6. Why is tipping based on a percentage of the sales price as opposed to the quantity of service rendered? For example, waitresses do as much work for breakfast as for dinner, yet receive far less in tips. Is this fair? Is it efficient?

7. Diners sometimes give money to the maître d' in hopes of getting a good table. Contrast this payment with a tip. Who has the upper hand? Contrast the bribe to the tip.

NOTES TO CHAPTER EIGHT

1. Amy Vanderbilt, *Etiquette* (Garden City, N.Y.: Doubleday, 1971).
2. Emily Post, *Etiquette* (New York: Funk and Wagnalls, 1965).
3. Vanderbilt, p. 851.
4. *Encyclopedia Americana*, 1973 ed., s.v. "Tip."
5. Post, p. 138.
6. Good Housekeeping, *Today's Etiquette* (New York: Harper & Row, 1965), p. 332.
7. Bureau of Labor Statistics, "Wages and Tips in Restaurants and Hotels" (Washington, D.C.: U.S. Department of Labor Bulletin 1712, 1970).
8. Ibid.
9. Department of Health, Education and Welfare, "Social Security and Cash Tips" (Washington, D.C.: HEW Publication No. SSA 72-10047).
10. Department of Labor, "State Laws under Minimum Wage and Orders Relative to Handling Tips on Gratuities as Part of the Minimum Wage" (Washington, D.C.: U.S. Department of Labor Publication #13355, 1965).
11. Vanderbilt, p. 882.
12. Post, pp. 105, 139.
13. Vanderbilt, p. 882.

Chapter 9

Scalping

BOX-OFFICE PRICING

Consider a monopoly that is selling tickets for a professional football game or a rock concert. It is assumed, for simplicity, that the number of tickets is fixed, and all seats are homogeneous. In figure 9-1, capacity cannot be expanded, and is given by Q_C. The demand for the particular event is DD. The profit-maximizing monopolist, unable to price discriminate and unconcerned with future sales or entry, sells that amount Q_O where marginal revenue equals marginal cost, charging price P_O. If price is set much lower, below P_C, demand for tickets exceeds supply. With no transactions costs, there is an incentive for scalping once official rates fall below this level.

In figure 9-2, with high demand relative to capacity, $P_O = P_C$, and a price the least bit below the profit-maximizing level creates excess demand, increasing the likelihood of scalping.

We can imagine scalping occurring in the real world even though there is no excess demand for tickets, even though the event does not sell out. For example, purchasers may be misinformed about the price or availability of tickets, or scalpers could conceivably offer their tickets at more convenient locations. Low box office prices, however, seem to be the principal cause of scalping.

A seller may price his tickets below P_C for a variety of reasons, including incompetence, internal institutional problems, non-profit-maximizing goals, or government decree. We assume that the official seller is a flexible, rational, unconstrained profit-maximizer. We also

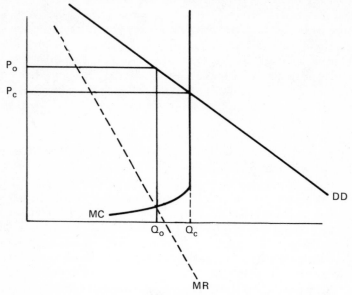

Figure 9–1.

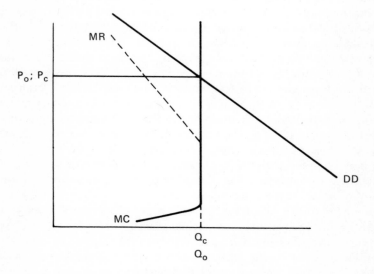

Figure 9–2.

assume, however, that there is some uncertainty with respect to the nature of demand.

If there is demand uncertainty, it is easy to understand why tickets are sometimes overpriced, sometimes underpriced. When demand is high relative to capacity, as in figure 9-2, we should often expect tickets to be priced so low (below P_c) as to create excess demand, and promote scalping. Real-world considerations generally cause the producer of an event to prefer to underprice rather than overprice his tickets.

The producer of an event is typically selling more than one item. A rock group expects its concerts to enhance record sales. The concerts (hopefully) shift audience preferences favorably, increasing the demand for the group's recordings. (The causation also runs in the opposite direction, with record sales changing preferences, and increasing the demand for concert tickets. The effects are mutually reinforcing.) Since profits from the albums are positively related to tour attendance, the maximization of total profits may mean the pricing of tickets below P_O in figure 9-1. Yet there is still no reason to charge prices below P_c, which sells out the arena, and in figure 9-2, the profit-maximizing price remains unchanged. However, when facing demand uncertainty, the rational seller should tend to underprice rather than overprice his tickets. Given high demand for the concert (figure 9-2), overpricing not only decreases profits from ticket sales, but also from the sale of records. In the spring of 1975, for example, the Rolling Stones released a number of new albums to "capitalize on the tour hysteria."[1] The hysteria might have been less if concert sales had been overpriced at $50 rather than underpriced at $10.

A rock concert takes time, and during this period there is a captive audience to whom other goods and services can be sold, such as programs, souvenirs, and particularly refreshments. Focusing on the sale of food and beverages, assume, for simplicity, that the desire for such general refreshment is unaffected by concert attendance. Attendance does, of course, increase demand for the particular food and drink provided at the concert. The ticket-seller monopolizes such sales only during the period of the concert and only for the captive concert audience.

A rational buyer should determine the total cost of both concert and potentially desired concessions before purchasing the ticket of admission. The profit-maximizing prices to be charged by the monopolist then depend on the interdependence and elasticities of demand. For example, the ticket-seller could conceivably charge a high price of admission while subsidizing the concessions. In the real world, the normal strategy seems the reverse. Concessions are generally priced quite high, while there may be an underpricing of admissions to attract customers to the arena. One reason for this strategy is that real-world customers are not perfectly rational, but tend to be a bit myopic, neglecting to include all related costs when making their ticket-pricing decisions. (Consumer myopia is apparent in other areas. For example, the prices of make-specific automobile replacement parts are large relative to cost. On the other hand, the new car itself may be priced a bit below the simple monopoly level to entice and lock in the potential buyer of replacement parts.)

Not only do entertainment producers sell a variety of complementary items, but they often create many similar events. A particular rock group's concert, for example, is generally performed in a number of cities, and sometimes a number of times in the same city. The quality reputation of a rock group becomes crucial in attracting fans to subsequent events. One indication of quality, among many, is past attendance. Continued sellouts indicate to potential ticket-purchasers that a particular rock group is in fashion, and may even be very good. Since buyers are more influenced by attendance than by total ticket revenue information, there is an incentive to set prices for a particular event below the short-run profit-maximizing level, P_o. (There may also be a temptation to inflate attendance figures. Witness the fledgling sports leagues.) And while there is no reason to price below P_c, if P_c is not perfectly known, the possibility of underpricing may be preferable to that of overpricing, especially if being "sold out" becomes an important informational variable for potential purchasers.

Let us draw together the argument thus far for the tendency to underprice. Even as we near capacity, extra revenue from selling one more ticket may be high compared to marginal cost (figure 9–2). We expect low marginal cost, since there is little expense in filling an available empty seat. In figure 9–2, overpricing loses a great deal of revenue, while saving only a small amount of cost. Moreover, overpricing can decrease net profits from albums, concessions, and future ticket sales. In contrast, underpricing is usually a less costly mistake. Only total revenue from current ticket sales decreases, though by a large amount (Q_c × amount of underpricing). In all, the rational seller, facing uncertain demand, may well prefer to underprice rather than overprice his tickets, thus increasing the probability of scalping.

In the real world, it is generally advisable for the monopolist to begin selling his tickets well in advance of the event. In terms of marketing, advance sales can make purchases more convenient, decrease buyer congestion problems, and allow early customers to better plan their lives by assuring them seats. Between the purchase of advance tickets and the time the event actually occurs, demand can be strongly affected by changing circumstances. The expected quality of a football game, for instance, may change sharply as weather forecasts are modified, or performers sustain or recover from injuries.

Adding the time element and the additional uncertainty created by changing conditions and information greatly complicates the analysis. Here we do not presume to thoroughly investigate the vast array of potential situations. Instead, a number of plausible assumptions are briefly mentioned that would tend to increase the likelihood of scalping in the real world.

If conditions turn out much better than expected, advance buyers could find scalping profitable. This is particularly true if the official seller were risk averse and preferred to sell a large number of advance tickets at well below the expected profit-maximizing price, in case the adverse contingency arose. In this latter situation, scalping becomes quite possible when favorable conditions occur. A ticket-seller may have other reasons for charging low prices for advance sales. For example, real-world capital markets being far from perfect, he might simply have an immediate need for cash.

Advance sales provide consumers with improved information about probable attendance. For many events, total attendance affects the utility an individual derives from the performance. A rock concert with tens of thousands attending is a happening; the same concert before five hundred may be a bust. There are, in other words, externalities in purchase. Your buying decisions affect my enjoyment of the event. If the externalities are positive, as in the example above, by changing expectations about actual attendance, high advance sales may increase demand, making a sellout and scalping even more likely.

It is possible to extend the argument farther. Consumers often gain utility from the envy of others. Once it becomes clear that the event will sell out and that excess demand exists, the expected utility from attending may be enhanced. Demand is again expanded, increasing still further the likelihood and profitability of scalping.

ECONOMIC EFFECTS OF SCALPING

Begin with the normal assumptions of the competitive model, but assume a monopolistic ticket-seller, who, for one of the reasons mentioned above, has set price at P_*, below P_c, so that excess demand exists ($Q_* - Q_c$). Tickets are sold on a first-come-first-served basis. For the moment, we assume that scalping is impossible.

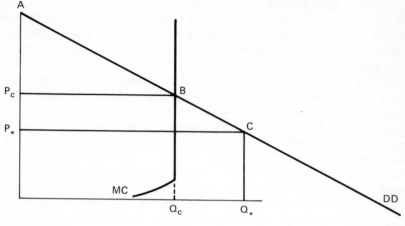

Figure 9-3.

Equilibrium is reached in this market by waiting. Though demand uncertainty was a principal reason the monopolist might price below P_c, we assume, for simplicity, that each individual buyer has complete and costless information about potential queues. No one makes a mistake by waiting, or not waiting, in line. In equilibrium, the total costs for the marginal individual, P_* plus his time costs, will be equal to (or possibly less than, if there is discontinuity) the total value he receives from the event. Neglecting income effects, as we do throughout the analysis, and assuming the arena is filled, this total cost per person must be less than or equal to P_c.

With queuing and nontransferability, an individual i will purchase a ticket as long as his dollar benefit from the event, U_i, minus his time costs t_i, are greater than or equal to the purchase price, P_*. $U_i \geq P_* + t_i$; we assume no one enjoys queuing up, so $t_i \geq 0$. The individuals who may buy a ticket are those on the demand curve from A to C in figure 9-3. No one below C will attend the event since $U_i < P_*$. While those people from B to C receive lower dollar utility from the event than do those from A to B, if they have very low waiting costs they may be the ones to purchase tickets. When compared to an ideal market there is inefficiency because some wrong people (from B to C) may be attending the event, and because any waiting can be considered a deadweight loss. Waiting generally creates costs for the consumer, without providing any benefit to the seller or to society.

The inefficiencies caused by waiting are due to the fact that no well-defined property rights exist for the underpriced tickets. Some of the available monopoly rent is dissipated,[2] as buyers use resources to establish claims to such rights. In the case at hand, time is employed in queuing to gain the right to purchase a ticket. Efficiency would be increased if cheaper methods of assigning property rights were employed. Since tickets are assumed to be nontransferable, it is also very important to assign the rights to the correct people.

If the property rights for access to tickets are arbitrarily assigned, then permitting the transferability of tickets will increase economic efficiency. Assuming no transaction costs for scalping, then customers A to B will attend the concert, which is the competitive result. Any costs in assigning property rights may be considered a deadweight loss. And any transaction costs in reselling tickets or property rights may prevent some of those with the highest dollar utility from viewing the event. For example, individuals B to C who receive property rights may prefer to attend the concert rather than to resell their tickets, should there be large costs associated with this transaction.

Contrasting situations of ticket transferability versus nontransferability when property rights are established by queuing is a more difficult exercise. Here we examine only a few simple possibilities, but show that allowing scalping can actually decrease economic efficiency. While the addition of markets generally enhances well-being, in this instance the negative externalities caused by waiting in line prevent such a facile conclusion.

The main efficiency problems caused by nontransferability and queuing are (1) that the "wrong" people may attend the event (those from B to C), and (2) the deadweight loss of waiting. Transferability combined with queuing lessens or eliminates the former inefficiency, but may increase the latter. Transferability, if there are no transaction costs, ensures that individuals A to B will wind up with the tickets. Transferability generally means that the total *time* spent queuing will increase; the total *cost* of queuing may be either higher or lower.

Without scalping, only individuals A to C are interested in waiting in line for tickets. Transferability makes potential waiters out of the entire population. Whether this increases or decreases the total cost of queuing depends on the situation. It would be necessary to know something about the time costs of the entire population A to Z, and the specific time costs associated with each individual A to C.

Many assumptions are possible. We assume that an individual's waiting costs are constant over time, and that there are no transaction costs in buying or reselling the tickets. Then, allowing scalping, and given no restrictions on how many tickets a single customer may purchase, theoretically a one-man line will emerge. This person can be expected to buy all the tickets for price P_*. He then becomes the monopolist and can resell the tickets, making a minimum monetary profit of $(P_c - P_*) Q_c$. He is the one in the entire population with the lowest time costs. If others had almost as inexpensive time costs, their competition would force him to arrive so early and wait so long as to dissipate most of his surplus.

Limiting sales of tickets to, say, one per customer would normally decrease the waste (still assuming no transaction costs). Given our assumptions, a line of Q_c people with the lowest time costs will form instantaneously some time before ticket sales begin. Since all have complete information about the queue, no one will arrive sooner, or wait longer. With no transactions costs, box-office sales are also instantaneous. Thus, everyone will wait the same length of time. The cost of waiting to the individual among those who value time most highly will not exceed $P_c - P_*$, the monetary gain from reselling the ticket. The surplus is dissipated only for the marginal individual. For all others, who value their time less highly, the benefits of possessing the ticket exceed their cost of waiting.

Nontransferability of tickets makes it quite unlikely that the total cost of waiting will reach $(P_c - P_*) Q_c$. Not only would all those in line need to have identical time costs, but the line would have to be composed entirely of individuals A to B. Given differing time costs, the surplus can only be dissipated at the margin. In such circumstances, the total waiting costs are less than under conditions of transferability and unlimited sales per customer, and may be less (or more) than such costs with transferability and one-to-a-customer sales.[3]

Let us elaborate, comparing one-to-a-customer sales with and without transferability. It might seem that by allowing tickets to be transferred, the number of potential waiters would be increased, and waiting costs decreased. Individuals A to B could hire waiters who place low values on time. If an individual in A to B had formerly waited himself, and now purchases the waiting services of others, doesn't his voluntary entrance into the transaction previously prohibited prove that he is now better off? The answer is No.

Let us assume that there are at least Q_c individuals C to Z with lower time costs than anyone in A to B. Their willingness to wait in line for long periods increases the cost to individuals A to B of waiting themselves. The length of the wait increases, and to get a ticket individuals A to B are forced to hire waiters at the competitive rate, which is $(P_c - P_*)$. This price turns out to be the highest any one of them could possibly have paid (in terms of waiting costs) under conditions of nontransferability, with only individuals A to C interested in waiting.

Without transferability, individuals A to C with low time costs would gain some of the potentially available monopoly rent (P_C - P_*) Q_C. With transferability, it is individuals C to Z who wait. They wait longer, but at a lower cost per minute. The cost to the marginal waiter among them is P_C - P_*. Others with lower time costs now receive some of the benefits of the monopoly rent. Whether the total costs of waiting would be more or less with or without transferability depends principally on the variability of time costs for those who wait in populations A to C, and in populations A to Z.

In the real world we often observe games and concerts that will eventually sell out not doing so immediately upon the opening of sales, or even within the first few days or even weeks. To explain this phenomenon, let us assume that buyers vary about when they make the final decision to attend the event, and about when it is convenient to purchase tickets. We also assume that there are transaction costs to every sale, and higher costs when buyers are forced to enter the market at inconvenient times. In such circumstances we can easily imagine that lifting the prohibition against scalping could make society worse off. With scalping there is a huge population in the market for buying the limited number of tickets, and we may find long early lines where none previously existed. The increased number of individuals who can conveniently buy tickets the first day of sales causes congestion and a deadweight waiting loss. Also, some of the individuals A to B who prefer purchases on the second or third day now find themselves induced to make early decisions, and perhaps arrive at the box office and wait in line at an inconvenient hour. Scalping increases not only the waiting and inconvenience but also the number of transactions and, thus, normal transactions costs. The total welfare of society is diminished. Though pure scalpers are made better off, many individuals from A to B are now much poorer, since they pay higher monetary prices for tickets, or wait in lines at times that are, for them, inconvenient.

MAIN DISTRIBUTIONAL EFFECTS
OF SCALPINGS

Consider a situation with perfect buyer information and excess demand, with tickets limited one to a customer and sold on a first-come, first-served basis. Allowing the transferability of tickets clearly benefits individuals C to Z with low time costs, permitting them to sell their time and earn a surplus. On the other hand, scalping may hurt some individuals A to C who had low time costs relative to others in that grouping, but not relative to the entire population. They do not wait themselves, and if they desire tickets, they must pay a larger premium in dollar terms than it would have cost in waiting time were scalping impossible. However, some individuals A to B with high time costs, who would not formerly have attended the event, are better off with scalping. And some individuals B to C with low time costs are better off if their waiting costs are increased by less than the added gain to be derived from reselling their tickets.

In general, scalping benefits some people C to Z, and can either improve or worsen the position of particular individuals A to C. Up to this point our analysis depicts scalping as having little effect on the profits of event producers. In the real world, of course, scalping may influence the timing and transaction costs of sales and the type of people attending the event, and thus the demand for concessions and other complementary items. But given our assumptions thus far, total ticket revenue for producers remains unaffected by scalping. We now consider a situation where scalping can seemingly decrease ticket revenues, where original sellers can profitably tie or bundle together different events.[4]

We assume perfect information. The seller produces a series of events, such as a season of football games. For simplicity we assume that there are two games, and stadium capacity is two. Marginal cost is zero up to two seats per game, and infinite beyond that. The four individuals with the highest reservation prices for the events are given below:

	Reservation Prices	
	Game 1	Game 2
Individual Alpha	$10	$1
Beta	9	6
Gamma	6	7
Delta	2	10

Pricing independently for each game, the profit-maximizing seller, unable to identify individuals, charges $9 for game 1, and $7 for game 2. Alpha and Beta attend the first game, Gamma and Delta the second. Total revenue is $32.

Let the seller bundle his products, offering the option of season tickets. Assuming the nontransferability of tickets, his optimal strategy is to provide season passes for $15, individual game tickets for $10. Beta purchases the season pass, and Alpha and Delta the tickets for individual games. Total revenue is $35; bundling is profitable.

	P_1	P_2	Season Pass	Total Revenue
Single Game Seats Only	9_A,B_	7_C,D_	—	$32
Season Tickets Included	10_A_	10_D_	15_B_	$35

Now allow scalping, at zero transactions costs. Individuals have an incentive to purchase two season tickets for $15. Epsilon (he is no fool) could resell them as single game passes for $32, making a $2 profit. With two season tickets being sold, total revenue for the event producer falls to $30. Scalping decreases the seller's prospective profits. He thus has an incentive to oppose scalping, and perhaps to make tickets nontransferable.

CONCLUSION

The strategy of ticket pricing is an intriguing subject. The first half of this chapter focused on only one aspect of this topic, explaining why, under conditions of uncertainty, tickets tend to be underpriced rather than overpriced. We argued that high attendance not only increases demand for complementary items, but also improves the seller's reputation for the future. Moreover, high advance sales can increase the likelihood of an exciting evening, favorably influencing other potential ticket buyers.

To simplify the analysis, the economic effects of scalping were examined under the assumption of perfect (buyer) information. This ignored the general uncertainty that may have given rise to the underpricing in the first place. But a fundamental conclusion was derived, that even under conditions of perfect information but excess demand, scalping might not prove socially beneficial. When tickets are underpriced and sold to competitive buyers on a first-come, first-served basis, scalping may increase waiting costs, and decrease well-being.

We have not made a case against either ticket transferability or scalping, but analyzed scalping only under a strict set of assumptions, ignoring many real-world costs and benefits. However, the telling theoretical point is that we cannot always be sure, by allowing additional markets, that we will definitely promote economic efficiency.

FOR DISCUSSION

1. Chapter Nine argues that allowing scalping might sometimes prove detrimental to society. Cite other examples where preventing the formation of certain markets could be the correct policy. Relate to the theory of the second best.

2. What do you think is the principal reason that many localities outlaw scalping? Is the scalper a nuisance? Are counterfeit tickets a problem? What pressure group might benefit from making scalping illegal? Explain.

3. If scalping is effectively prohibited, can a case be made for also banning transferability? Should student athletic participation cards be transferable? Why or why not?

4. Do consumers have a notion of a "just price"? Would fans be outraged if World Series tickets were priced ten times higher than the regular season entry fee? Do pennant winners underprice their Series tickets to protect goodwill? (How can you tell if tickets are underpriced?) Is rationing by waiting a more equitable method than rationing by price? Explain.

5. Cite some circumstances or events where audience satisfaction is positively correlated with attendance. In such situations, would spectators really subsidize others to attend? Could this be arranged practically?

NOTES TO CHAPTER NINE

1. "Stones Loom, Tickets Boom," *Rolling Stone* (19 June 1975), p. 15.
2. Yoram Barzel, "A Theory of Rationing by Waiting," *Journal of Law and Economics* 17(April 1974):73-95.
3. This conclusion stands in sharp contrast to that reached by Steven N.S. Cheung "A Theory of Price Control," *Journal of Law and Economics*, 17 (April 1974):69.
4. For an excellent article on bundling, see William James Adams and Janet Yellen, "Commodity Bundling and the Burden of Monopoly," Harvard Institute of Economic Research Discussion Paper Number 402 (February 1975).

✳ *Part III*

More Micro Applications

Chapter 10

Insurance

There is an old vaudeville song, sung by a poor man, which argues that money doesn't mean a thing to a person's mental state. After all, "a man with seven million is as happy as a man who has eight." An economist would agree with the spirit of that verse. In economics jargon, since the law of diminishing marginal utility holds for most goods and combinations of goods, it also holds for money. As money income increases, each new dollar adds something to utility, but total utility grows at a slower and slower rate. The extra amounts of goods, services, leisure, or security that can be bought with the additional money contribute less and less to satisfaction.

The diminishing marginal utility of money means that individuals will tend to be risk-averters. Given the option of taking a large, actuarially fair bet versus not gambling at all, most people will choose not to gamble. Who would bet his entire income, double or nothing, on the flip of a coin? While it is sometimes enjoyable to make small bets, few people are willing to stake significant portions of their wealth on a game of pure chance.

Risk aversion makes people willing to pay something to reduce the risk of loss; the larger the potential loss, the more they will pay. Consider a situation where an individual owns a house, valued at $100,000. Ninety-nine other individuals own similar houses, and it is known that one of these one hundred homes will be totally destroyed this year. When the year ends, each homeowner has a 99 percent chance of having a $100,000 house and a 1 percent chance of having nothing. Assume that there is no danger of personal injury. Rather than face the possibility of large loss, most individuals would prefer to enter into some risk-spreading arrangement. Each could agree to pay $1000 into a pot, with the $100,000 going to that unlucky individual whose house has been destroyed. Everyone would thus convert the 1 percent chance of a $100,000 loss into a certain, but much smaller loss of $1000. If the homeowners were true risk-averters, they would be willing to pay somewhat more than the $1000. There thus may be room for a profit-making insurance company to exist, whose expenses and profit can be met out of the higher premiums.

An insurance contract can be considered an exchange of today's money for the guarantee of larger amounts to be returned in the future *if* some generally unfortunate contingency occurs. The purpose of insurance is to reduce risk by converting large uncertain losses into smaller but certain premiums. Since insurance generally entails high administrative expenses, it doesn't make sense to insure against minor losses. These are better handled through savings.

While insurance usually covers against large losses, the insurance company itself may not be taking on great risks because what is somewhat unpredictable for the individual is often highly predictable and uniform en masse. The homeowner does not know which particular houses will be destroyed this year, but the insurance company can estimate the percentages relatively accurately. Generally speaking, spreading the risk reduces it. For the insurance company, the larger the number of policies, the less the risk *if* the occurrence of the adverse events are largely independent. When they are positively correlated, increasing the number of policies may actually increase the insurer's risk. For example, it may not be wise for a single company to insure more and more homes in any particular valley against flood, or more and more San Franciscans against earthquake damage.

Interdependent contingencies constitute just one of the problems that worry insurance companies. Two others, of great interest to the economist, are termed "adverse selection" and "moral hazard."

ADVERSE SELECTION

A private health insurer is, in effect, betting with each policyholder that he will not get sick. The insurance company can get excellent average data on what percentage of a large group of similar individuals is likely to become ill. But each individual may know more about his own particular susceptibilities than an insurance company can easily find out. For example, the individual usually has better information about his own family's medical history.

Since insurance premiums tend to reflect the average level of risk for any category, those people within groupings whose own risks are greater than the average are likely to be attracted by the good bargain the insurance represents. Conversely, those who know that their own risk is below the average are less likely to purchase the insurance. The worse risks tend to buy insurance, while the better risks do not. An excellent example of this phenomenon of adverse selection occurs with pregnancy insurance; those who intend *not* to have children are less attracted to the policy, while those planning a family tend to enroll. The insuring of primarily high-risk families forces premiums to rise, which further reduces the number of insureds.

Another area where adverse selection occurs is in the used-car market. While buyers may be able to discover the average quality of specific make/model cars on the market, any potential seller should know a great deal more about the quality of his own particular automobile. Product information is again asymmetrically distributed in the market, but here the sellers know more than the buyers. At any given market price for a specific make/model, those potential sellers with cars of lower quality will be more attracted into the market, while those with higher quality cars will be less likely to enter. Adverse selection occurs. The average quality of cars in the market falls, and so does price.[1]

Several methods are used to deal with the problem of adverse selection. Insurers can try to gain more information about the product, such as by requiring medical tests before issuing health or life insurance. They can make narrower and narrower groupings for different classes of insurance, lessening the variance within each group, and thus the magnitude of the adverse selection problem. Ideally, each buyer could be put in a separate category representing his particular risk.

The adverse selection problem is that relatively too few low-risk (high-quality) individuals become insured. Fixed and compulsory coverage, as is required of some aspects of automobile insurance, solves the problem. In voluntary plans, it helps if the cost of insurance is kept low. Group plans tend to be less expensive because of lower administrative and selling costs. The income-tax laws also promote group insurance: rather than the individual paying for coverage out of already-taxed take-home pay, the employer is allowed to pay for coverage tax free. This decreased cost makes it more likely that low-risk individuals will purchase the group insurance.

MORAL HAZARD

A second major problem faced by insurers is that having insurance often changes the individual's incentives and decisions. This is the "moral hazard" problem. The term does not usually imply moral perfidy, although it may, as when an arsonist burns down a building for the insurance. Instead, the phrase generally denotes rational economic behavior when prices change. The problem for society is that private rational choices are not always socially rational.

Owning insurance influences a person's behavior in two principal ways: it makes the individual less careful in avoiding, or preventing the danger, thus increasing the likelihood that the catastrophe will occur; and it increases the insured's demand· for replacement and repair goods and services.

Consider the example of home fire protection. A rational individual should ask himself, how much fire protection apparatus should I buy, how safe against fire should I make my house? The economist's answer is that the homeowner should buy another unit of fire protection (e.g. thicker walls, less flammable fabrics, better fire extinguishers) as long as the extra benefit is greater than the extra cost. The individual's demand for fire protection will be downward sloping: the lower the price, the more he will demand. As price falls, he will increase his purchases and his protection.

What is the effect of owning home fire insurance? The insurance, by decreasing the individual's loss from fire, will decrease his demand for fire protection. Assume for simplicity that the only danger is property damage, and that the fire creates no inconvenience. If the insurance pays for the entire loss, a fire destroying an individual's home affects him only to the extent that it may raise everyone's premiums. Therefore, the demand for fire-protection equipment falls. In the initial example of the one hundred homeowners, it falls by 99 percent. If we being from a position of optimality, insurance means that there will be too little concern for fire protection, and too many fires.

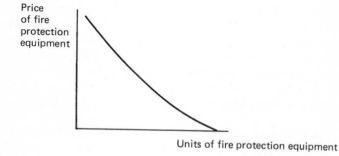

Figure 10-1.

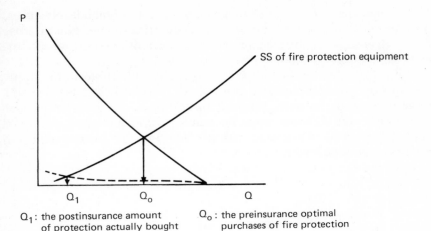

Q_1: the postinsurance amount of protection actually bought

Q_0: the preinsurance optimal purchases of fire protection

Figure 10-2.

If there are no fire externalities (e.g., other houses burning) then the marginal social benefit of preventing a $100,000 home from burning down is $100,000. Without insurance, the extra benefit to the homeowner from avoiding a fire is also $100,000. But with insurance, this figure drops to $1000. The owner now receives only 1/100 of the benefit from protecting his own home. The other ninety-nine insureds receive the rest. From the social perspective, each individual has an incentive to purchase too few safety options.

Consider an owner who has the option of buying a device that will decrease the chance his home will burn down from 1 percent to 0.25 percent. Without insurance, he would pay a minimum of $750 for the device (more if he is risk averse), or .75 of 1 percent times $100,000. With complete insurance, the device is worth only about $7.50, or .75 of 1 percent times $1000. No one will buy the device if it costs much more than this, and too many homes may burn down.

Insurance tends to make people more negligent, careless, and less health and safety conscious than optimal. This is one aspect of the moral hazard problem.

Insurance also tends to induce individuals to demand more and higher quality goods and services for replacement or repair. If we begin with perfect competition, the insurance causes a divergence from the Pareto optimal solution. We will discuss insurance for hospitalization since that is one area where the moral hazard problem has caused severe efficiency losses in recent years.

Consider a simple insurance plan that will pay 80 percent of all medical fees. Without insurance an individual has some demand curve for medical care; the higher the price, the less he demands. However, once he becomes insured, he pays only one-fifth of the total or gross price. Given this fall in price, he will demand more and higher quality services.

The effect is much like an 80 percent subsidy. If we think about the subsidy going directly to the patient, this will shift his demand curve upward by fivefold. Without insurance, if the price per unit of health care was $10 per unit, he would demand X units. Now the price can be $50, the insurer will provide $40, the insured will pay $10 and still demand the same X units.

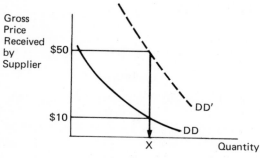

Figure 10-3.

Alternatively, if we wanted to think that the insurance is paid directly to the producer, we could argue that the supply curve will fall by four-fifths. Note that on the vertical axis now is net price paid by the patient, rather than gross price received by the supplier. Without insurance, when the net price paid by the patient was $100, only Y units would be supplied. With insurance, the consumer need only pay $20, the insurer will contribute $80, the producer will receive the same $100/unit and will supply Y units (figure 10-4).

In the health-care field, the rapid increase in private and government insurance coverage has caused a dramatic increase in demand and prices. The increase in coverage has increased demand, and since long-run supply has not been highly elastic, prices have shot up drastically. Between 1950 and 1975, direct hospital payments by the patient have fallen precipitously, from 35 to 10 percent. During the same twenty-five years, as the consumer price index has risen by 122 percent, the hospital price index has increased by 700 percent.[2] Wherever possible, patients are not only demanding more medical care, but also care of higher quality. To make matters worse, the skyrocketing medical prices have forced more individuals to seek more

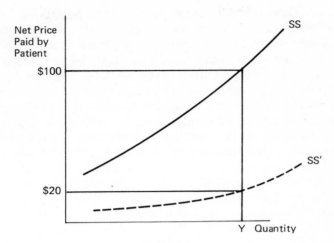

Figure 10-4.

complete medical coverage, thus exacerbating this moral hazard problem.

Consider a perfectly competitive world, and add health insurance. The insurance acts like a subsidy, and with any elasticity in demand and supply curves, causes individuals to consume too much medical care. Any individual is not sufficiently motivated to restrain his own use, since while he receives the total benefit (assuming, for simplicity, that there are no externalities), the cost is spread over others. The new demand (or supply) curves do not reflect marginal social benefit (or marginal social cost). And price, quantity, and quality of services consumed are too high from the viewpoint of society. There is allocative inefficiency. Society could be better off if fewer resources were devoted to health care, leaving more available for other areas.

A related moral hazard problem is that as insurance coverage increases, the patient has less incentive to shop around for the best bargains. Hospitals are thus permitted a higher effective profit, or are allowed to survive even though grossly inefficient.

There are a variety of measures designed to alleviate the problems of moral hazard. To increase care, insurers may lower premiums to policyholders who take precautions. There is an added incentive to exert caution if auto insurance costs fall as one's driving record improves. And there is a greater incentive to buy less damageable cars if this reduces insurance premiums.

Coinsurance and deductibles help increase precaution and decrease overuse. Coinsurance means that the insurance covers less than 100 percent of all expenses. In other words, the insured is forced to pay a fraction of all costs. This fraction (20 percent in our medical-care example) should be low enough to avoid financial calamity, but large enough to reduce the moral hazard problem. Deductibles are equivalent to 100 percent coinsurance (or 0 percent insurance) for small repairs. For example, the first $100 or $200 of car repairs must often be paid by the insured. A principal purpose of deductibles is to avoid the administrative cost of small claims, but they also provide a financial incentive that encourages precaution, though not one that inhibits demand once the deductible limit has been passed.

Indemnities provide a method that virtually eliminates the problem of overuse. Instead of covering a certain percentage of costs, indemnity insurance provides a *fixed*-sum payment for loss. While indemnities usually cover losses where replacement is difficult or impossible (e.g., loss of life), they could be used to protect against a variety of risks. Their major limitation is that when damage and replacement expenses are variable, a fixed lum-sum payment generally leads to over- or underinsurance.

Careful monitoring of replacement and repair expenses is another method by which insurers seek to control the moral hazard problem. So too are prepayment schemes, such as are used by health maintenance organizations. In HMOs the client pays an insurance premium and can receive reimbursement should he become ill. But instead of cash, payment is in kind. It is the supplier who receives a type of fixed indemnity payment, which gives him an incentive to provide efficient, though perhaps less extensive service.

CONCLUSION

The law of diminishing marginal utility holds not only for most goods, but also for money, income, and wealth. Thus, there is a demand for insurance against large losses, even though administrative expenses may be high. Of course, some large risks cannot be insured against; the prime examples concern events over which the potential insureds have great control, such as business failure. Those businesses seeking such insurance would know they had a high likelihood of failure; and once insured, they would have much less incentive for success. These are the problems of adverse selection and moral hazard.

Adverse selection and moral hazard create problems for insurers and for society. Adverse selection is caused by the buyer's greater knowledge of whether or not the unwanted contingency is likely to occur. If inadequate information forces insurance companies to group lower and higher risks together, the lower have less incentive to purchase coverage. Such individuals, though they may want insurance, find the price too high. The dynamics of the situation could worsen the problem as insurers are forced to raise premiums, driving even higher risk purchasers out of the market.

The problems of moral hazard are caused by the changed prices faced by the insureds. Insurance against catastrophe makes people (rationally) more careless, increasing the likelihood that the catastrophe will occur. And insurance that pays for replacement or repair increases demand for such products and services. These moral hazard effects not only create problems for the insurer, but also reduce economic efficiency.

FOR DISCUSSION

1. If people are generally risk averse, why do so many gamble? Does it ever make sense to match quarters? Why or why not?

2. The adverse selection problem occurs in the market for insurance and for used cars. Give another example of a market where adverse selection may exist.

3. Does a single insurance company have much of an incentive to promote safety? Does the insurance industry? Explain.

4. Since a fire at one's house may damage other homes, will individual decision making lead to the optimal amount of private fire protection? Does insurance ameliorate or aggravate the problem?

5. "Not enough houses burn down." Could this statement ever be true? Can houses ever be too well protected against fire?

6. "Auto insurers have discovered that people settle for smaller amounts in cash than in repair services, because they always want the smashed left door to look as good as new if somebody else pays for it, but are often happy to get it banged back into workable shape for $50 if they can pocket $100 in cash."[3] Comment. Relate to moral hazard.

7. Explain the major differences between the market for health insurance and the market for property insurance.

8. Carefully explain the inefficiencies caused by adverse selection.

9. What is the purpose and effect of the tax advantage to employers contributions to group insurance plans?

NOTES TO CHAPTER TEN

1. George Akerlof, "The Market for 'Lemons': Quality Uncertainty and the Market Mechanism," *Quarterly Journal of Economics* 84(August 1970):488-501.

2. Mark Pauly, "Health Insurance and Hospital Behavior," in Institute for Contemporary Studies, *New Directions in Public Health Care* (San Francisco: Institute for Contemporary Studies, 1976), pp. 103-29.

3. Thomas C. Schelling, "Medical Care Guarantees: Economics of Choice," in Institute of Medicine, *Implications of Guaranteeing Medical Care* (Washington, D.C.: National Academy of Sciences, 1975), p. 28.

OTHER SOURCES

Kenneth Arrow. *Essays in the Theory of Risk-Bearing* (Markham, 1971), chapters 5, 8, and 9.

Mark Pauly. "The Economics of Moral Hazard," *American Economic Review* 58(June 1968):531-39.

Paul Samuelson. *Economics* (New York: McGraw-Hill, 1976), appendix to chapter 21.

Chapter 11

Externalities

As chairman of the Arrangements Committee, you are responsible for the organization and success of the class party. Your conception of a successful party is one where everyone consumes large quantities of alcohol, but you also want to be assured that proceeds from the party will just cover costs. How do you go about pricing drinks?

A cash bar, where people pay by the drink, is one possibility. A much superior alternative from your perspective is for the class as a group to agree to share alcoholic costs equally. After the party, the total cost of drinks will be divided by class size, and all will pay an equal assessment. This arrangement covers costs, and it also increases consumption.

Let us examine a simple numerical example. There are fifty students in the class. Drinks are homogeneous (for instance, beer) and cost the committee 50¢ per glass. A typical individual's demand curve for drinks is given in figure 11-1. The higher the price he pays for a drink, the less he consumes. At a cash bar, with drinks priced at 50¢, he buys Q_0.

Now consider the alternative arrangement. Each member of the class has agreed to share all alcoholic costs equally. An individual deciding whether or not to have another drink realizes that the cost to him is only 1¢. The forty-nine other members of the class each bear a 1¢ cost for his drink. In figure 11-1, the marginal private cost curve has fallen to 1¢. A rational individual consumes Q_1, consuming more as long as the extra utility or benefit to him is greater than 1¢. The underpricing has caused him to increase his consumption.

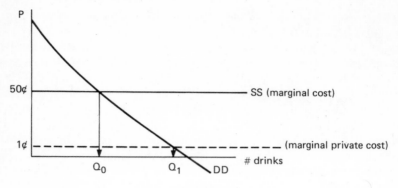

Figure 11-1.

A similar situation occurs in many localities with the pricing of another liquid—tap water. A community demand curve for such fresh water is given in figure 11-2. There are costs to the community of supplying water to each household: the cost of purifying and transporting the water, as well as the possible cost of decreased swimming and boating pleasures if lakes are turned into reservoirs. The marginal social cost is given by MSC in figure 11-2.

With marginal cost pricing, A units of water are consumed. But many localities do not charge the user anything for water. The costs are instead born by the entire community, via taxes. If the community is large, any individual will perceive the cost to himself of consuming another unit of water as being virtually zero. Individuals will become wasteful of water, leaving the tap on, not fixing leaky faucets, etc. Consumption increases to B, past the point where the

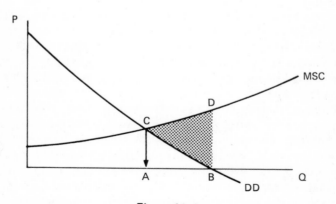

Figure 11-2.

marginal benefit from an additional unit of water exceeds the marginal cost.

Figure 11-2 gives a measure of the efficiency costs of this underpricing and overconsumption. Ignoring income effects, the extra benefit of consuming B rather than A units is given by the area within triangle ABC; the extra cost is given by quadrangle ABDC. The social cost of overconsumption is therefore represented by the shaded triangle BCD.

In both of these examples there are externalities; the individual consumer does not bear the full cost of his consumption. The marginal private cost of another drink of water or beer is unequal to the marginal social cost. Decision-makers do not take sufficient account of the costs they impose on others. Their decisions are not optimal from the viewpoint of society.

The problem of pollution is similar. The cost of pouring impurities into the air or water is usually not fully borne by the polluter. The polluter imposes costs on others, but these costs are not sufficiently represented in the polluter's cost/benefit calculus. The private cost—the negative price for producing this "bad"—is not large enough. Hence, acting rationally, following his own self-interest, the decision-maker tends to overpollute.

In equilibrium, perfect competition ensures that the amount produced or consumed of each commodity for every decision-maker is at a level where the marginal private benefit = (price) = marginal private cost. An externality occurs when the marginal *social* benefit is unequal to the marginal private benefit, or the marginal *social* cost is unequal to the marginal private cost. For example, if you play the jukebox, this may enhance (or detract from) others' pleasures; if you catch the flu, you may infect others; if you attend the basketball game, it may increase fan excitement; if you remodel your home, it may boost neighborhood land values.

(There are also external effects when a new product decreases the profits of firms in competing industries, or changed preferences decrease the demand for one product and increase it for another. But these are pecuniary externalities, externalities that affect others not directly, but through the price system. Pecuniary externalities are not discussed here for they do not prevent perfect competition from achieving Pareto optimality in long-run equilibrium.)

Direct externalities cause nonoptimal amounts of goods or bads to be produced and consumed. One could view this as a pricing problem; production or consumption of the commodity is at a level where marginal social benefit ≠ price, and/or marginal social cost ≠ price. Economists thus often favor "internalizing" the externality as a method for correcting the inefficiency. This means charging the decision-maker with the costs he imposes on others, or rewarding him with the benefits.

Assume, for example, that figure 11-3 gives the demand and supply schedules for competitively produced studded snow tires. The supply curve represents the marginal cost in terms of real resources used (land, labor, and capital) to produce another snow tire. The demand represents the extra utility of another snow tire to the next highest bidder. In a world of perfect competition and no externalities, $P_0 Q_0$ represents not only equilibrium price/quantity, but also the Pareto optimal result for the given distribution of resources. However, studded snow tires create externalities. They ruin roads, which create additional costs for others: less comfortable rides, shorter auto life, and increased taxes for road paving and repair. We might say that the supply curve does not include all the costs of another studded snow tire. People rationally following their own self-interest buy too many.

Let us make a heroic simplification and assume that each studded snow tire creates the same extra cost, $10 per tire. The externality could then be easily internalized by requiring studded-tire buyers to pay the cost they impose on society. An excise tax of $10 per tire would shift up the supply curve to reflect marginal social cost. Equilibrium price would then equate marginal social benefit and marginal social cost, and decrease output to the optimal level.

Note that the externality problem would not arise if each individual drove only on his own property. Then any damage done would be borne entirely by the decision-maker, and marginal private cost would have been equivalent to marginal social cost.

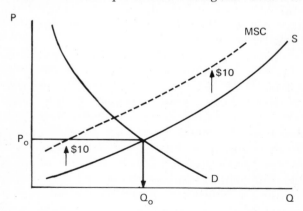

Figure 11-3.

PROPERTY RIGHTS

The absence of well-defined and easily enforceable individual property rights is one of the fundamental causes of externalities. In the city-water example, imagine a number of fresh ponds to which residents go to gather water. The water is owned by the public collectively, and it is distributed on a first-come, first-served basis, at zero price. As population and demand grow, a point is reached where the marginal social cost exceeds zero. One citizen's drawing of water forces others to do without, or to trudge to more and more distant ponds. There is overconsumption. In order to achieve efficiency, government must begin marginal cost pricing. If there are large numbers of small ponds, private ownership of each by competitive water suppliers could achieve the same result automatically. Each tiny supplier would face a horizontal demand curve and would profit maximize by producing where P = MC.

Efficiency problems will also occur if particular oil fields are under multiple ownership and control. Under law, the oil belongs to the firm that brings it to the surface. While there is a maximum efficient pumping rate, this will usually be exceeded, since it does not pay for any individual firm to exercise restraint while his neighbor captures more than his share of the resource. Competition for the oil in any paticular field leads to too many holes being drilled and too rapid pumping, resulting in a loss of natural pressure and a greatly reduced total oil yield. The problem may be decreased by government regulation, but unitized management of each field eliminates the inefficiency without government interference. If there are large numbers of oil fields, unitized management also allows the existence of a competitive oil market.

The rule of capture also applies to common fishing areas, leading to the killing of too many and too small fish. The problem is that no one owns the fish while they are in the water, and a single fisherman does not bear the full cost he imposes on society. Killing fish increases the cost to other fishermen by decreasing the current and future numbers of fish available. Without some common enforceable agreement, an individual fisherman has little incentive to refrain from catching fish, even relatively young fish, in order to increase next year's yield. He has no guarantee that others will also refrain, or that his own action will have more than a negligible effect. His restraint benefits all fishermen, but he himself receives only a small portion of the benefit. But all fishermen would be better off if all exercised restraint.

The situation can be depicted by a prisoner's dilemma game (see appendix). Any single fisherman's profits depend in part on the actions of other fishermen. Each individual acting purely in his own self-interest will disregard the effects of his actions on other fishermen. He wishes others would exercise restraint, but his own dominant strategy is not to. If all act in their own self-interest they will reach a dominated outcome. All would be better off if all exercised restraint, but each has an incentive to cheat. They would thus like some method to help them collectively achieve the preferable result.

Theoretically, there are a variety of methods to eliminate the problem of overfishing, including catch limits, taxes to internalize the externality, or attempts at unified management, especially for nonmigratory fish such as salmon, cod, or haddock. Current methods of making fishing vessels technologically inefficient seem less desirable. Virginia oystermen, for example, are required to employ cumbersome twenty foot tongs to raise oysters laboriously from public waters, instead of using efficient dredges towed by motor boats. In Maryland dredges can be used, *if* they are towed by *sail*boat, except on Monday and Tuesday, when motorized pusher-boats are permitted.[1]

Why may whales, buffalo, deer, alligators, lions, and hawks be in some danger of extinction while pigs, camels, horses, goats, cats, and goldfish are not? The fundamental explanation seems to be the absence, or presence, of property rights. There is great difficulty in owning the former animals, domesticating and breeding them. They are wild. Ownership is determined by the rule of capture, a type of first-come, first-served arrangement. A nineteenth-century American

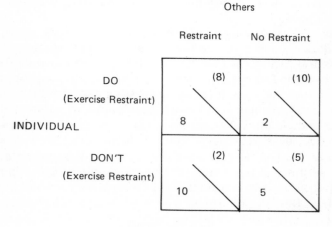

Figure 11-4.

hunter had little incentive to refrain from killing buffalo; if he didn't kill them, someone else would. Too many buffalo were destroyed, virtually eliminating them from the American scene. The prisoner's-dilemma model is applicable here. Individual hunters did not take into account the costs they imposed on others, especially the Indians.

On the other hand, there is little need to worry about the extinction of pigs. Pigs are privately owned. An owner receives virtually all the direct benefits and costs when a pig is destroyed. He has no incentive to wantonly kill his own pigs, and no one else is allowed to. If the pig population were to fall suddenly (because of disease), then ceteris paribus, the value of each pig would increase, creating an incentive for farms to try to increase pig production.

PUBLIC GOODS

The examples so far have focused on rival goods, where one person's consumption of a particular item eliminates the possibility for others to consume it. Pork is a rival good; if one person owns and eats the meat, another cannot also eat it. By contrast, public goods are nonrival goods. Enjoyment by one individual in no way detracts from use or enjoyment by others. Flood control, military defense, and lighthouse signals are common examples. While individual demand curves for rival goods are added horizontally to obtain market demand, individual demand curves for public goods should be added vertically. For example, if the one hundred million households that would be protected by an increase in defense spending would be willing to pay $10 for another unit of missile defense, this unit is worth at least $1 billion (100 million × $10) and should be produced if it costs less than this amount.

A second aspect of pure public goods is that noncontributors cannot be excluded from the benefits. Thus, no one has an incentive to pay for the public good unless compelled to. This is the "free-rider" problem, and is the reason why public goods are provided publicly rather than by private entrepreneurs. No one has an incentive to pay for a dam if he will receive its protection whether or not he contributes. The prisoner's-dilemma game illustrates the problem. Each person has a dominant strategy not to contribute (*don't*), but wishes everyone else would contribute. All could be better off if all, rather than no one, contributed. The typical solution is to agree collectively to require everyone to contribute through taxes.

Private decision making will not provide the optimal amount of public goods. However, there are often methods of making the goods less public by devising ways of excluding noncontributors, of eliminating the free riders. Thus, a lighthouse could send out only coded signals on selected frequencies, with only financial supporters having knowledge of these. Or defense against crime in the streets (police protection) could be provided only for those with special badges indicating voluntary contribution to the defense program. But such methods eliminate only the free-rider aspect of public goods, not their nonrivalry. Their nonrival nature means the marginal cost of providing the service to another individual is zero, and hence any exclusion, even if possible, is inefficient. However, if the service is to be profitably provided by private organizations, some sort of exclusion is usually necessary.

The classic western movie *High Noon* is a drama built around the public goods/free-rider problem. Gary Cooper as sheriff learns that an outlaw leader he sent to jail has been released, and will arrive on the twelve o'clock train to be met by his terrorist gang. Coop seeks aid from the townsfolk, but while each desires defense—"so that decent women and children can walk the streets"—this benefit will be available to anyone whether or not he stands with Cooper at high noon to face the outlaws' guns. The townsfolk, given little time to collectively mobilize, end up hiding. The one early volunteer quickly deserts when he learns that there is no one else willing to help; his likelihood of dying has become too high. Cooper also has great incentive to leave town: his term as sheriff expires the next day; his Quaker bride threatens to leave him; the townsfolk have deserted him; and his chance of survival is low—all of which makes his decision to stay and his ultimate victory the more heroic and incredible.

PERVASIVENESS

Economist Tom Schelling tells of the time his two-year-old son, looking out the window, asked his father "Why are all the other houses on the outside, when ours is on the inside?" While microeconomics usually focuses on situations where all nonpecuniary costs and benefits are internalized, real-world situations almost always involve interesting and important externalities. Social interaction, for example, is virtually all "externality." If you are not Robinson Crusoe, almost everything you do affects others in positive or negative ways. A smile, a friendly hello, a pat on the back brings utility to others; how you eat, what you wear, with whom you associate matters to other people. Chapters 3 and 4 on fashion and social forces discuss some of these externalities.

Most of society's laws can be viewed as attempts to channel private behavior in such a way as to promote the public interest. Fines for walking on the grass, littering, or double parking try to internalize the disutility such actions can impose on others. Prohibitions against murder and assault have the clear purpose of deterring conduct that can cause enormous unhappiness to others.

Many of society's customs and codes of ethics are also designed to help make the invisible hand work. The social rules concerning reciprocity in gift and social exchange promote beneficial transactions while maintaining part of their spontaneity and voluntarism. Such conventions as the handshake, the bow, and the "excuse me" keep interactions friendly. The golden rule is a prime example of a code of conduct, which, if everyone followed it, would make everyone better off.

CONCLUSION

An externality is defined as an action that brings direct benefits or costs to others, but these do not sufficiently enter into the utility calculus of the decision-maker. There are probably some externalities in most actions you take, including washing the dishes, wearing new clothes, walking the dog, driving a car, or having a child. The importance of the externality depends on a large number of factors.

Where there are externalities, private decision making may not lead to the social optimal. From the social perspective, too much or too little of an activity will be undertaken. A variety of methods can improve the situation, including the changing of ownership patterns, taxes and subsidies, regulations, laws, social sanctions, and moral imperatives. Which, if any, is most appropriate depends on the specific situation.

FOR DISCUSSION

1. Is it proper to force people to get polio inoculations?

2. What is the rationale for government allocation of the radio spectrum?

3. What is the reasoning behind urban renewal? Why won't individual owners improve their property to gain higher rents? Why don't individual families have the responsibility of maintaining their own cemetery plots in large graveyards?

4. Why do we need zoning laws?

5. Are people more careless with library books than their own books? In public parks than in their own backyard? Why?

6. How do communes get people to work their fair share?

7. After all the talk about democracy, why do so few people vote in the U.S.?

8. Why weren't the buffalo wiped out by the American Indian before the advent of the white man?

9. Will private decision making lead to the optimal population size?

NOTES TO CHAPTER ELEVEN

1. Tom Alexander, "American Fisherman are Missing the Boat," *Fortune* (September 1973), p. 244.

OTHER SOURCES

Garrett Hardin. "The Tragedy of the Commons." *Science* 162(1968 December 13):1243–48.

Mancur Olsen. *The Logic of Collective Action.* Cambridge, Mass.: Harvard University Press, 1965.

Thomas Schelling. "On the Ecology of Micromotives." *The Public Interest,* Number 25(Fall 1971):59–98.

Chapter 12

Crime

Have you ever broken the law? There are many ways to do it. To name but a few crimes, there is murder, assault, rape, robbery, burglary, larceny, arson, manslaughter, kidnapping, and hijacking; there is extortion, embezzlement, fraud, forgery, counterfeiting, bribery, perjury, and plagiarism; there is adultery, bigamy, incest, indecent exposure, prostitution, and obscenity; there is smuggling, espionage, desertion, and treason; there is vagrancy, truancy, drunkenness, and disorderly conduct; there is impersonating an officer, parole violation, and prison break; there is unlawful assembly, obstructing justice, and inciting to riot; there is hunting, driving, or practicing without a license; there is speeding, double parking, hitchhiking, and jaywalking; there is gambling, loan-sharking, and dealing in drugs; there are housing code violations, blue law violations, and discrimination; there is child abuse, tax and draft evasion, suicide, sale of stolen goods, aiding and abetting a fugitive, illegal immigration, insider dealing, smoking in an elevator, and vandalism.

Most of us have committed offenses that could land us in jail. One suggestive though nonrandom self-report survey of one thousand adult males found that 64 percent were unarrested felons, having engaged in such activities as grand larceny (13 percent), auto theft (26 percent), assault (49 percent) and burglary (17 percent). Of lesser crimes, 84 percent of respondents admitted to malicious mischief, 85 percent to disorderly conduct, 57 percent to tax evasion and 36 percent to criminal libel. A typical adult male had committed some eighteen offenses![1]

Although many of us have committed crimes only a small portion of us have been arrested or imprisoned. It is thus probably incorrect to draw a sharp distinction between "them" (the criminals) and "us" (the good guys). Of course, the high recidivism rate for serious crimes such as robbery indicates that some of us commit more serious crimes than do others.

Most criminals are similar to normal people. Studies show that lawbreakers are no more likely to have a certain stature, to be feeble-minded, or to suffer from a psychosis.[2] Economists postulate that criminals are generally as rational as law-abiding people. The economist assumes that a man who steals does so largely because he has different opportunities and perceives different costs and benefits compared to one who doesn't. Believing that criminals are not fundamentally different than other people, economists include both their and their victims' utility when considering the welfare effects of crime.

Economists can bring a variety of insights and anlytical tools to the study of the complex phenomenon called crime. Public finance economists are trained to analyze the optimal allocation of resources —among various enforcement tools, among different locational districts, among various crimes, and between law enforcement and other activities. Industrial organization economists can discuss the black market for illegal goods and services; the relationship between market size and theft; why some crimes are organized while others are not; and why some legitimate industries are more susceptible than others to incursions by organized crime. Fraud, deception, and swindling can be analyzed, as well as other white-collar crimes such as violations of the antitrust or pollution-control laws. Labor economists can deal with racketeering, the effects of unemployment and labor-force participation on crime, as well as the problem of the released offender. All the subdisciplines of economics can contribute to our understanding of crime, including economic history (e.g., the effects of prohibition), urban economics (e.g., city size and crime), international economics (e.g., smuggling), and radical economics (capitalism and class struggle as part of the problem).

The economist is trained to analyze a myriad of issues in criminology. This essay examines two, the economic costs of theft, and the economics of black markets.

THE COSTS OF THEFT

When most people discuss the costs of theft, they emphasize the amount stolen. But to an economist, this amount merely represents a transfer of wealth. If Peter takes $15 from Paul, Paul is $15 poorer, but Peter is $15 richer. There are clearly equity, ethical, and moral issues involved, but in terms of efficiency, we cannot conclude that the before-theft situation is (Pareto) superior to the after-theft result. If Paul is sweet, kind, virtuous, and perhaps poor, while Peter is rich and horrid, we may be justifiably angered by the theft. But if we refuse to make interpersonal comparisons, as is normal in welfare economics, we cannot rank the two situations. Moreover, there is no way to further redistribute wealth to make *both* prefer that the theft had or had not occurred. Therefore, at first blush, one might conclude that there are no *efficiency* problems with theft.

On further thought, however, there appear to be a number of potentially large efficiency losses associated with stealing. Let us abstract from the immense possible disutility caused by physical harm, or the fear of harm that may accompany theft, and consider situations where there is no meeting or communication between thief and victim (or bystanders) and no fear of future physical harm.

One efficiency problem caused by theft is that if property rights cannot be easily safeguarded, less than the optimal amount of property will be produced. Figure 12-1 gives the demand and supply curves for bicycles in a competitive market, with theft impossible. Given perfect competition, $P_0 Q_0$ represents equilibrium price and quantity, as well as the optimal amount of bicycle production and purchases given the initial distribution of income. Now let bicycles be stolen from users. The demand curve will shift down to DD' in the diagram. (If bikes are stolen from suppliers, the supply curve will

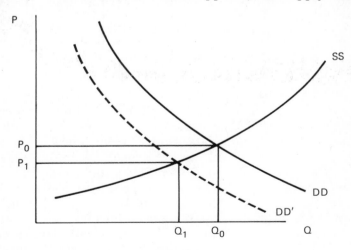

Figure 12-1.

shift up.) The expected utility of the bicycle for purchasers is now less since they may lose the bike to thieves. The new equilibrium P_1Q_1 is not optimal, for P_1 understates the true value of bicycles—the value or utility of the bicycle for the thief is not included. If the thief were required to purchase the bike, the price would truly represent the marginal social benefit of the last bicycle provided. But with theft in this market, too few bicycles are produced and consumed. The more likely bicycles are of being stolen, the more the demand curve shifts down, the fewer bikes are produced, and the greater the allocative inefficiency.

A social cost of theft is that both the thief and the potential victim use resources to gain or maintain control over property. Both parties use capital and labor in the struggle to secure property rights. In a broad sense, this struggle may be called a "transaction cost." The thief spends time and money in his attempt to steal (he buys wire cutters), and the legitimate property owner expends resources to prevent the theft (he buys locks). These costs may escalate as a type of technological arms race unfolds. A bank may purchase more and more complicated and sophisticated safes, forcing safecrackers to invest further in safecracking equipment and education.

A related cost of theft is that it forces changes in decisions, lifestyles, and perceptions. A bank may not be able to open at the most convenient times or locations if this unduly encourages theft. A bike-owner may find it too risky to leave his bike in certain locations, and may sometimes be reluctant to use it at all. Crimes can be most destructive if they alter attitudes unfavorably. People may become distrustful, and less likely to emote goodwill and compassion; they may be less willing to aid strangers. Some of the community spirit that helps keep crime low and the quality of life high may be lost.

BLACK MARKETS

Many transactions between willing participants are or have been outlawed, for a variety of reasons. The loaning of money at usury rates is banned in most states. So is the selling of cigarettes to minors or the hiring of illegal immigrants. Dope, prostitution, gambling, and pornography are also illegal, as is the exchange of contraband or stolen goods. At times in the United States the sale of liquor, gold, abortions, contraceptives, and ration coupons has violated the law.

It is policy that creates black markets. We currently forbid certain narcotics but not tobacco, gambling in casinos but not on the stock market, extramarital sex but not gluttony, erotic stories but not mystery stories.[3] Someday we may permit homosexuality while banning firearms. Here we examine some of the major economic consequences of the illegality of marijuana.

With no government interference, the market for marijuana might approximate the model of perfect competition. There could be many small manufacturers, wholesalers and retailers, easy entry, and good information about prices and product quality. Figure 12-2 denotes the free market demand and supply curves for this chemical.

Suppose now that the government makes marijuana *consumption* illegal for all its citizens. It slaps a large fine on any citizen smoking or otherwise consuming marijuana; selling marijuana is still permitted (perhaps because sales to foreign tourists are considered desirable.) What is the effect on price and quantity consumed?

A citizen's demand now becomes wrong and risky. The simple fact that the good is now illegal will probably decrease most people's desire for the weed, though it may increase a few people's demand. The risk of being caught and fined decreases virtually everyone's demand. The demand curve thus falls. At the same market price less is demanded; or alternatively, a lower price is required for consumption to remain the same. As shown in figure 12-3, equilibrium price and quantity have decreased.

Now consider an alternative enforcement scheme. Possession and consumption are permitted, but growing and selling are prohibited. There are now higher costs of production: the cost of paying fines, of bribing the police, and of producing and selling in less efficient ways, but ones that decrease the likelihood of detection. The supply curve shifts up and to the left. At any market price, less will be supplied; suppliers now require a higher price to supply the same amount. Figure 12-4 shows the effect on equilibrium price and quan-

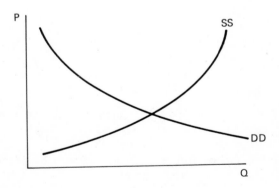

Figure 12-2.

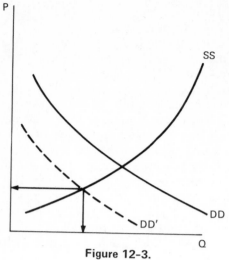

Figure 12-3.

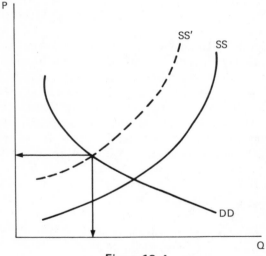

Figure 12-4.

tity. Market price rises as quantity falls. Outlawing a commodity generally decreases output, but depending on the enforcement scheme, market price can either rise or fall.

An enforcement policy directed at the supply side decreases information availability. Advertising is made exceedingly difficult; brand names are hard to establish; liability or fraud suits may be impossible. The lack of buyer information tends to increase price and quality variation among sellers. It also tends to decrease average quality by increasing the likelihood of successful adulteration. Illegality also decreases quality by forcing suppliers to use less detectable methods. This can be most readily perceived in the case of prostitution, where the possibility of discovery by police makes it less profitable for sellers to invest heavily in plush surroundings.

What are the costs and benefits of keeping marijuana illegal? The principal benefit is that it decreases consumption. This benefits those who favor the law. They derive utility from having others not smoke. The user himself may benefit if the law helps him in his desire to avoid and resist the temptation. If marijuana were addictive or associated with other social problems—theft, poor driving, assault, insulting behavior, inability to support one's family, heroin addiction—the benefits would be larger and more apparent.

The costs of the illegality include a higher price and lower quality for those who want to consume, law-enforcement expenditure and costs (including jail sentences), and increased disrespect for law. The costs (and benefits) of making desired transactions illegal are probably larger for many other commodities: the illegality of abortions decreases their quality, thus mutilating more women; the illegality of prostitution decreases its quality, increasing the likelihood of venereal disease and the robbery of clients; rising heroin prices due to illegality increase the need for addicts to steal to feed their habit; liquor and gambling bans helped establish organized crime. The magnitude of these costs, combined with a belief that the individual is generally the best person to know what is good for himself, leads many economists to advocate the decriminalization of most of the so-called victimless crimes.

FOR DISCUSSION

1. "People seldom plant apple trees where passers-by can easily take apples even if the value of the apples to society would exceed the costs" (Alchian and Allen, *Exchange and Production*, 1969, p. 244). Comment. Relate to the costs of theft.

2. Why do many buses now require exact change? Is this a cost of theft?

3. The thief and the potential victim are struggling over property rights. Compare this to the situation where goods are underpriced and distributed on a first-come, first-served basis. (See Chapter Nine, "Scalping.")

4. What would be the effect if, instead of outlawing pot, the government granted a monopoly to a particular seller? What if the monopoly were granted annually, and given to that firm willing to pay the government the most money for the right to produce and sell?

5. Blackmail is a (somewhat) willing transaction between a seller and a particular prospective buyer. Why is it illegal? What would be the economic effects of legalizing it?

6. Why is it illegal to sell your vote?

7. What would be the major economic effects of making it illegal to possess a firearm?

8. The fewer people that are out walking the street at night, the less safe it is to be walking around at night. Will the optimal number of people be out?

9. On the average, exconvicts are less reliable than other employees. But hiring excons reduced their likelihood of returning to a life of crime; it reduces the recidivism rate. Will the free market provide jobs for the right number of excons? Would governmental policies be helpful?

NOTES TO CHAPTER TWELVE

1. James S. Wallerstein and Clement J. Wylie. "Our Law-Abiding Law-Breakers." *Probation*, New York: National Probation Association, 1947.
2. Edwin H. Sutherland and Donald R. Cressey. *Principles of Criminology*, 7th ed. (Philadelphia: J.B. Lippincott, 1966.
3. Thomas C. Schelling. "Economics and Criminal Enterprise." *The Public Interest*, No. 7 (Spring 1967).

OTHER SOURCES

Armen A. Alchian and William R. Allen. *Exchange and Production*. Belmont, Cal.: Wadsworth Publishing Co., 1969, chapter 12.
Gordon Tullock. "The Welfare Costs of Tariffs, Monopolies and Theft." *Western Economic Journal* 5(June 1967):228-31.
A.J. Rogers. *The Economics of Crime*. Hinsdale, Ill.: The Dryden Press, 1973, chapter 4.

✳ *Part IV*

Industrial Organization

INTRODUCTION

Macroeconomics focuses on the performance of the economy as a whole. The concern is with such aggregate measures as gross national product, unemployment, and inflation. Business economics focuses on the individual business unit, explaining the internal working of the firm and prescribing ways for it to achieve greater efficiency, sales, and profits. Between macro- and business-economics lies microeconomics, which examines the functioning of markets. Microeconomics does not describe how individual actors can enhance their own position in the economy, but how, from the viewpoint of society, market performance can be improved.

Industrial organization is an important branch of microeconomics. The basic concern is industry performance, viewed from society's perspective. (Is the right quantity of goods being produced? the correct number of varieties? Are the products produced efficiently? Is there the optimal degree of innovation and progress?) The fundamental theory of industrial organization is that market structure (the number and size distribution of buyers and sellers; the ease of entry of new firms into the market) affects market conduct (the amount of advertising; whether there is collusive behavior among sellers, etc.), and that both affect market performance. Public policy issues addressed by industrial organization economists include antitrust (should particular firms be allowed to merge? should price leadership be attacked?) and regulation (what rules should the Interstate Commerce Commission prescribe? what is the optimal patent policy?

should doctors be licensed? are mandatory car safety standards desirable?).

The four chapters in this section fall under the rubric of industrial organization. The first examines an important, but vague, aspect of market structure: product differentiation. It explains some of the problems inherent in this concept and discusses the effects of product differentiation on other aspects of market structure.

Chapter 14 deals with a related, but neglected topic: grading. It emphasizes that grades are not a datum, but are usually the result of conscious decisions; describes some important effects of the grading of goods in the real world; and helps explain why some goods are graded while others are not.

Since industrial organization theory has its foundation in static price theory, there is a tendency among economists to ignore dynamic market events. The third topic concerns one such short-run phenomenon often excluded from consideration: business exits. Chapter 15 explains the benefits and costs of exit and examines evidence from the United States experience.

The final chapter describes the old New York ice trust, which attempted to monopolize an industry initially characterized by many small buyers and sellers, easy entry, and a homogeneous product. This chapter gives a glimpse into the seamy side of business behavior at the turn of the century, and applies simple industrial organization analysis to this fascinating real world case study.

Chapter 13

Product Differentiation

ELEMENTS OF MARKET STRUCTURE

In the model of perfect competition, every market is characterized by many small buyers and sellers acting independently, easy entry and exit, a homogeneous product, and excellent product and market information. There are no externalities. As a form of applied price theory, industrial organization focuses on departures from the competitive model. Thus, the three aspects of market structure generally stressed by industrial organization economists are: seller and buyer concentration, barriers to entry and exit, and product differentiation. Less attention has been paid to other market structure characteristics such as demand growth, the price elasticity of demand, or the durability and perishability of the product. These are probably less crucial. In applied price theory they are important only if the market is already imperfectly competitive.

Of the three principal market structure characteristics, concentration is the most straightforward. There is a minor issue in determining the best measure of concentration, but the main theoretical and practical problem is defining the market when goods are not homogeneous. Still, workable approximations can be made, and reasonably decent data on seller concentration in American manufacturing industries are published by the Department of Commerce. Economists do not emphasize the buyer's side of the market as much as the seller's side, since low concentrations are more prevalent and recognized interdependence among buyers is less likely. Moreover, information about buyer concentration is not so easily obtainable.

The entry barrier concept is more elusive than is concentration. Not only is there the ubiquitous problem of market definition, but a legitimate question exists as to why an ultrasharp distinction should be drawn between firms with small sales in the market and those with none at all (possible entrants). Theoretically, the most useful way of defining barriers (barriers measure the advantage of which established firm(s) over which potential entrant(s)?) is not entirely clear. But it is the *practical* measurement problems that overshadow all others. Empirically, either sophisticated guesses of high/medium/low barriers, or very crude proxies such as economy of scale estimates are used. Economists are generally less concerned with barriers to exit, perhaps because they appear less important in our growing economy.

Product differentiation is the third major aspect of market structure. Products within an industry are said to be differentiated if buyers have nonidentical preferences among the competing outputs of various sellers. These preferences can be due to virtually any cause (perhaps other than a price differential). Product color, size, design, quality and packaging are sources of product differentiation, as are firm service, location, and reliability. It is only necessary that differences be perceived; they need not be actual.

As seller concentration and barriers to entry correspond to deviations from the competitive model of many small sellers and easy entry, product differentiation encompasses many of the problems caused by product heterogeneity and incomplete or costly information. Heterogeneity per se, of course, does not insure product differentiation. Buyers need both to perceive differences and to care about them. Even then, if all buyers rank goods identically, this may result in a kind of grading rather than product differentiation. (If coal were valued solely for energy and type A coal had twice the energy content of type B, it would sell for twice as much. If the price differential increased, all buyers would switch to type B coal. Small producers of type A and type B coal could thus face perfectly elastic demand curves, indicating no product differentiation.)

Incomplete information per se is neither necessary nor sufficient to insure product differentiation. Indeed, the inability of buyers to distinguish among actually heterogeneous products could prevent product differentiation from arising. Yet product differentiation advantages are often associated with incomplete buyer knowledge. Brand names are beneficial largely because they provide information, reducing the search costs of purchasers.

Though the concept is rarely used, it seems logical to mention product differentiation on the buyer's side of the market. Sellers may have preferences concerning to whom they sell. During the gas shortage, for example, regular customers often received favored treatment. Established borrowers sometimes gain preferred lending rates or, more often, access to funds unavailable to others. Drug-pushers like to sell to regulars in order to decrease the possibility of inadvertently dealing with undercover narcotic agents. In all these cases sellers can distinguish certain buyers and, for a variety of reasons, prefer to deal with them. While the concept of product differentiation can be used to describe these examples of established and valuable reputations on the buyer's side, for simplicity, this chapter will follow the normal usage of generally identifying product differentiation with the seller's side of the market.

PROBLEMS OF DEFINITION AND MEASUREMENT

The concept of product differentiation as an element of market structure is an amorphous one. First there is the enormous problem of market definition, for if goods are not homogeneous, there is no precise way of delineating the industry. There is also an interesting qustion as to whether an industry containing only one seller, or only one buyer, could be structurally characterized as being product differentiated. The answer seems to depend on the specific definition one chooses to employ. The conventional description of product differentiation is too vague to be of much help.

It is usually argued that the way to distinguish markets characterized by product differentiation, and to determine the *degree* of product differentiation, is to look at demand elasticities. Both own price elasticity and cross-price elasticity are suggested. The competitive model provides a standard for comparison in either case. In perfect competition, each firm faces a completely elastic demand curve. Products in the same market are perfect substitutes, the cross-elasticities infinite. The existence of product differentiation (1) makes firms' own demand curves less elastic, and (2) decreases intra-market cross-elasticities.

Even at the theoretical level, there are severe problems in using demand elasticities to measure product differentiation. In pure monopoly there is no cross elasticity among firms in the industry —there is only one firm. And the own price elasticity of this firm depends on *inter*industry substitutes. In oligopolistic markets, a single firm does not face a unique demand curve. Own and cross price elasticities depend on rivals' current prices, prices which are not technologically determinable. Even in atomistic markets there are problems. Own and cross-elasticity measure may differ, and it is not obvious which is the more useful. More important, both are really firm indices, and no single method of cumulation stands as *the* correct way of calculating the industry measure.

Indeed, one reason the concept of product differentiation is vague is because the term is often used, and may be more suitable, as a firm rather than an industry variable. It seems obvious, for example, that General Motors had a product differentiation advantage over Kaiser-Frazer (though there is no conventional method of measuring it). However, it is far from clear whether product differentiation in the automobile *industry* increased or decreased with the demise of th smaller auto firms.

Another potential problem with using demand elasticity to measure product differentiation is that it ignores what may be an important consideration: the allegiance of particular buyers to particular sellers. Elasticity measures involve static analysis, while often implicit in the discussion of product differentiation is a time element, whether particular buyers tend to stick to the same seller, or switch over time. However, while many business economists feel that this is inherent in the concept of product differentiation, we might better consider brand loyalty as a measure of its microstability.

The theoretical problems of measuring product differentiation are, of course, nothing compared to the empirical difficulties. Approaches used include advertising as a percentage of sales, an entropy or inertia measure (the extent to which customers make their continuing purchases from the same seller), and high/medium/low subjective evaluations. It is obvious that none of these is very good.

How useful would it be to be able to measure product differentiation accurately? What major predictions could be tested? First, product differentiation can affect performance directly. In monopolistic competition, more product differentiation may mean sellers face less elastic demand curves, and, ceteris paribus, there will be higher prices and probably more firms and more excess capacity in the long run. (The ceteris paribus includes no change in entry barriers.) In tight oligopoly, decreased cross-elasticity of demand could allow higher profits, generally decreasing allocative efficiency. The direct effect on other performance variables such as technical efficiency of progressiveness is less certain. One possibly important influence, ignored in static price theory, is the effect of product differentiation on the severity of certain disequilibrium problems. It is sometimes claimed that a firm's product differentiation advantage can act as a beneficial buffer against short-run shocks.

Product differentiation also affects market performance indirectly through its effects on market structure and conduct. Product differentiation influences, and is influenced by, certain forms of business behavior, most notably advertising and other forms of selling expense. Its relationship with particular elements of market structure is described in more detail below.

REPUTATION: ITS RELATIONSHIP TO
SIZE OF BUYERS AND SELLERS,
AND TO ENTRY BARRIERS

One of the problems in discussing product differentiation is that the term encompasses so much. This section lumps a number of important sources of product differentiation under one heading: *reputation*, by which is meant such aspects as quality assurance and reputation for reliable delivery and dependable service. While the distinction is not clear-cut, factors like product design and firm location receive less emphasis. The accent is upon those elements of product differentiation that are built up over time.

Reputation matters when buyers have less than perfect information. Since much of the cost of acquiring product information is independent of purchase size, there are generally economies of scale in buying. Large purchasers usually get better information than do much smaller ones. Large firms have specialized purchasing agents who buy by specifications. At the other extreme are individual households, who, lacking hard data, are more easily swayed by Madison Avenue. Though reputation is not unimportant in producer goods industries, it is in consumer goods markets, where buyers are small, that brand names, reputation, and product differentiation matter most.

The structure on the seller's side of the market can affect buyers' ability to gain product information. Buyers get product information from a variety of sources, including their own previous experience, contact with other users, and through trade journals or magazines like *Consumer Reports*. Generally, the older and larger any particular seller, the easier it is to gain information about its products. There have been more users of the product in the past, the product is more likely to have been tested by a Consumer's Union, and its durability and repairability tested by time.

A normal way of gaining useful, though biased product information is directly from the manufacturer or seller. Large current and potentially future sales generally give advantages here, since there are often increasing returns to selling expenditures. In consumer advertising, for example, a certain saturation level is often necessary before the ad campaign reaches maximum effectiveness. In addition, large advertisers may be granted volume discounts.

The large, established seller should thus generally enjoy some product differentiation advantages over others in the industry. There are some scale economies in direct information dissemination, and it is easier for buyers to discover the reliability of the large firm. Moreover, when firms are large, they usually have a great incentive to maintain reasonable product quality. They are conspicuous, information about their poor performance is more quickly disseminated, and they have a large investment in reputation to protect. Buyers know this and can more safely depend on the self-interest of the large established firm to protect them. (Of course, since expert purchasers can more easily detect poor quality or fraud, they need less to rely on the large seller's investment in brand reputation. It is to be expected that, ceteris paribus, small sellers will face less of a disadvantage when buyers are expert.)

Though perhaps unmeasurable, the potential reputation advantage seems likely to increase monotonically with relative market size. In other words, a General Motors may possess a slight differentiation advantage over a Chrysler simply because of its larger sales volume. Any consumer relying on word-of-mouth advertising will probably come across more GM users. Moreover, since there are more GM dealers, he will probably be more closely situated to one. Buyer search costs are thus generally less for the GM product.

The reputation advantage of large firms is generally greatest in relationship to new entrants. This represents part of the product differentiation barrier to entry discussed by economists. If there are buyer information costs, they should be greater for the products of new than of established firms. Entrants thus face a current absolute cost disadvantage in terms of information dissemination.

Most of the reputation advantage of the established firm can be considered as caused by past investment in "goodwill," due to past advertising or perhaps simply due to past existence and performance. Failure to properly include these investments in calculating profits may sometimes give established firms an illusory advantage over new entrants. For example, counting advertising as expense rather than as investment decreases current profit figures while it inflates future returns.

A truer reputational advantage would be caused if it were more difficult to differentiate a new product in the face of already established brand names. The market environment for new entrants may be dramatically altered after a few firms gain major reputations. It may be harder, for example, to sell a Kaiser to a previous Ford buyer than to a man who has never owned an automobile at all, or particularly to a man who has never heard of the Ford Company. Certain forms of buyer behavior can be hypothesized that would create a reputational advantage to "getting there first." This would in part explain the observed willingness of firms to accept early losses in order to establish a foothold in the market.

Entrants may face a further reputational disadvantage if, for any of a number of reasons, their market share remains small compared to existing rivals. A completely new firm, for example, may face customer differentiation disadvantages in attempting to borrow money; or organizational growth problems may penalize very rapid expansion. Also, the past investment in product differentiation by existing firms inhibits massive market entry, keeping new firms small and imposing further reputational disadvantages from such sources as word-of-mouth advertising.

CONCLUSION

Though the term *product differentiation* is part of the economist's everyday vocabulary, the concept is a highly amorphous one. The term is employed both as an industry and a firm variable, and in neither case is there a clear method of even theoretical measurement. Empirical proxies are generally far from satisfactory.

This chapter focused on one aspect of product differentiation, labeled broadly as reputation, and discussed some of the relationships between reputation and firm size and entry barriers. Emphasis was placed on the fact that reputation is partly influenced by past sales volume, thus giving the large established firms some advantage over smaller firms or new entrants in the market. Put another way, there are externalities in purchase. What you buy not only can affect what is available to me, but also the cost of acquiring information about that product. The argument is that your purchase of a Volkswagen decreases my costs in determing the quality of a VW.

Like product differentiation, reputation is also a vague concept. This chapter did not examine it in detail, nor did it explore the *importance* of reputation in enhancing sales, or the *importance* of past sales in enhancing reputation, or the use of devices such as guarantees that may lessen reputational disadvantages. The relationship among the various methods buyers use to gain product quality information also was not given close scrutiny.

However, some interesting theories and explanations arise from even our cursory discussion. The general high quality of major brand names, for example, can be explained by the firms' desire to maintain their reputations, although there are occasions when the lure of short-run profits may lead to quality deterioration. The generally high quality is in terms of "inspection" and especially "experience" characteristics, aspects about which the buyer can readily gain information from the past experience of previous users. For other characteristics, quality need not be so high. The reputation problems for certain aspects of automobile safety, for example, were never great. It was difficult for an individual driver to accurately determine car safety; also, no one kept good statistical records.

Another theory concerns the chain of distribution. Given an independent chain, we might hypothesize that the longer it is, ceteris paribus, the larger the potential reputation advantage of established firms. Since every stage along the chain must be persuaded to purchase the new item, the more stages there are, the more problems facing a new entrant. This means that the potential for product differentiation at the manufacturing level for consumer goods may be greater than at the retail. The argument may not be completely convincing, but it could be tested empirically.

FOR DISCUSSION

1. How would you go about determining whether one firm had a product differentiation advantage over another? How could you deduce whether one industry was more structurally differentiated than another? Does the concept of product differentiation make more sense as an industry or a company variable?

2. Do you expect brand names to be more important for buyers when goods are purchased in large or in small volume? For goods that are bought regularly or irregularly? Are products or services more likely to be characterized by product differentiation?

3. What product differentiation advantages might a large established *steel* firm have over a potential entrant? Over a small steel firm?

4. Why is it easier for a firm to keep old customers than to attract new ones? Explain a new entrant's strategy of initially offering a very low price, and then gradually raising it.

5. If all aspirin is chemically identical, how can Bayer sell at three times the price of A&P aspirin? Does this mean that buyers are irrational? If GM wanted to make aspirin available for all its employees on the job, would it buy Bayer?

6. How *important* are reputational advantages due to past sales? When deciding on a new car purchase, does it matter whether or not a 1965 Chevrolet was a good car?

7. To the extent that firm size is important for product differentiation advantages, is this a real (social) or pecuniary (private) benefit of scale?

8. "The denial of copyright liquor labels during prohibition meant that only the bigger gangs would guarantee the quality of their liquor and hence assisted them in developing monopoly control of the business" (Thomas C. Schelling, *The Strategy of Conflict* [New York: Galaxy paperback, 1963], p. 137). Comment. Relate concentration and product differentiation to the likelihood of fraud, whether or not contracts can be legally enforced.

9. In discussing product differentiation, economists make the caveat that identical buyer preferences will lead to implicit grading. But is this always the case? Consider a number of industrial purchasers, buying an essential product from a small number of sellers. Not only is the product homogeneous, but the sellers are exactly alike, save for one small particular. Though they use identical types of men, machines, and material, they do not share the very same ones. Might not it therefore make good sense for any buyer to spread his purchases, for fear of the equally likely but somewhat independent possibility of machine failure, wildcat strike, etc. at the plant of any one specific supplier? Buyers could then have identical preferences, but any supplier might be able to raise his price without losing all sales.

Comment. Is this product differentiation? What if there were large numbers of sellers?

SOURCES

Irwin Bernhardt and K.D. MacKensie. "Measuring Seller Unconcentration, Segmentation, and Product Differentiation." *Western Economic Journal* (December 1968).

Richard Caves. *American Industry: Structure, Conduct, Performance.* Englewood Cliffs, N.J.: Prentice Hall, chapters 2 and 3, 1972.

Edward H. Chamberlin. *The Theory of Monopolistic Competition.* Cambridge, Mass.: Harvard University Press, chapter 4, 1962.

George Day. *Buyer Attitudes and Brand Choice Behavior.* New York: Free Press, 1970.

Richard Heflebower. "The Theory and Effects of Nonprice Competition," in Robert E. Kuenne, ed. *Monopolistic Competition: Studies in Impact.* New York: John Wiley, 1967, pp. 177-201.

James Koch. *Industrial Organization and Prices.* Englewood Cliffs, N.J.: Prentice-Hall, chapter 11, 1974.

Robert H. Nelson. "The Economics of Honest Trade Practices." Draft, 1972.

Chapter 14

Grades

Classification and grading of goods are often mentioned together. Classification generally refers to the dividing of a commodity into lots which have uniform characteristics, without implying either superior or inferior groupings. Thus, wheat is sometimes classified by variety, honey by color, potatoes by size, and beef by sex. Within classifications, grading is often performed, categorizing the commodity as to quality. Grades for honey include "fancy" and "standard"; beef is graded as "prime," "choice," and "good."

There are many potential competitive repercussions from the grading of goods and services. This chapter discusses some of the principal effects of grading, especially with respect to scale advantages, and tries in general to explain why grading occurs where it does.

SOME EFFECTS OF GRADES

The principal economic benefit of grades is in the provision of information on product quality. Grading is one way of supplying such information, a substitute and sometimes complement for other methods such as advertising, brand names, and guarantees. Grading differs from these particular alternatives in being an industry-wide rather than a firm-specific method of providing information. Products of differing sellers are ranked by the identical grading system.

A common grading system increases the ability of buyers to purchase without personal inspection, thereby facilitating transactions at a distance. Grades can also help to eliminate fraud, to expedite the financing of loans to producers and middlemen, and to ease the determination of insurance claims.

Grades provide for all buyers the same neat summary appraisal of product quality. Thus, grades not only help to make buyers better informed, but also lead them to rank products similarly. Introduction of grades therefore tends to eliminate some of the product differentiation advantages of established sellers, making their demand curves more elastic, and generally lowering barriers to potential entrants.

There are usually scale advantages in quality assurance. Over some range, the average cost of assuring quality declines as direct assurance expenditures increase. For example, a certain size advertising budget is required to gain access to national TV or to hire the services of well-known independent testing laboratories. Perhaps more important, the average cost of assuring quality also declines for the firm as quantity sold increases. When a particular brand or company has high past and present sales, a potential purchaser finds it easier to obtain "testimonials" from friends, buyer magazines, etc., and is more likely himself to have had experience with that brand. In other words, quality information about the product is cheaper to obtain. Grades, by providing information to buyers, tend to eliminate some of these scale differentiation advantages. Grades thus permit the small seller to compete more effectively. One consequence of meat grading, for example, may be to reduce seller concentration in that market. It is not surprising that established firms with product differentiation advantages are often the strong opponents of new grading schemes.

Many other effects of grading might be mentioned. Grading, for example, may decrease the scale advantages of larg-scale *buyers.* Some of the scale economies that exist in purchasing are caused by the fixed costs of obtaining product quality information. Large firms are often able to employ full-time purchasing agents; they can write their own specifications and buy by them. In contrast, smaller concerns and final consumers are forced to rely more heavily on advertising and brand names. Government grading and testing of products provides much quality information and helps eliminate one of the advantages the big purchaser has over the small.

Like any measure, grades may change man's perceptions and incentives. Aspects of quality that are heavily weighted in a grading system will tend to be emphasized, while those receiving less weight may tend to be neglected. It is sometimes argued that grades will have the effect of making goods more homogeneous. To the extent that quality is "standardized," this could make oligopolistic coordination easier, and cheating on implicit or explicit price-fixing arrangements simpler to detect. It is also claimed that grades could inhibit beneficial technological innovation. Finally, there are the direct costs of grading, which may sometimes be large.

GRADED AND UNGRADED GOODS

Commodities actually graded in the United States include milk, eggs, wool, lumber, mushrooms, soybeans, meat, scrap iron, and diamonds. As should be expected, major brand names are generally not important in such markets, and small firms face few product-differentiation disadvantages. Additionally, graded commodities are often those for which existing firms might have had difficulty in establishing quality assurance advantages, and therefore where resistance to grading was probably least. A usual feature of currently graded products is that their quality does not predominantly depend on "factory control" procedures, but on more unpredictable factors, often on nature. The number of knots in a given piece of lumber, for instance, is a somewhat stochastic variable, and is largely independent of the ability or efficiency of the producer.

Graded commodities are probably those where there was little resistance to grading by established firms. From the social perspective, it might be argued that these were the most desirable candidates for grading. The commodities are often produced by many and scattered firms; thus, grading could provide great assistance to buyers, for a large number of geographically dispersed sellers usually makes search costs high. Grades are also most helpful to purchasers when other information substitutes, such as strong brand identifications, do not exist. And the fact that the commodities were often primary goods made them more amenable to grading. Their primary nature made it easier to discover some generally agreed-upon rank ordering, and their "God-made" property lessened the potential problem that the grades might inhibit major design breakthroughs.

Since grades generally tend to decrease the value of built-up reputation and trade names, firms possessing certain product differentiation advantages often resist attempts to initiate a grading system. Major paper companies and automobile tire manufacturers, for example, have long opposed grades for their products. The established firms usually claim that their products are not suitable for grading. Among other things, they argue that the goods possess many noncollinear but highly important product quality characteristics. Absorbency, softness, and strength are all important aspects of paper towels, and it may depend on use or preference whether an absorbent weak towel is considered superior to a strong but less absorbent one. Consumers, of course, might still benefit if *each* of the product attributes were graded, or if complete grades could be given by product *use*.

A second major argument of those opposed to grading is that grades may focus competition on the wrong areas. Certain characteristics of writing paper, such as appearance, formation, printability, and lack of curl presently defy accurate measurement. Producers claim that if the setting of definite standards for the measurable characteristics is carried to extremes, this would tend to limit manufacturers in developing some of the unmeasurable characteristics that are often far more important. The argument is that the information provided may prove misleading, and that purchasers may actually be made worse off than had they received no grade information at all.

While grading is not practical for all products, for many, grades might provide cheap, useful, and succinct quality information. Commodities currently graded seem ideal for grading, and it is difficult to discover cases where the grading should be stopped. On the other hand, inadequate buyer power combined with the reluctance of established sellers to relinquish brand advantages may combine to prevent the creation of other potentially beneficial grading systems.

CONCLUSION

Where goods are graded, grades written, and products tested by some competent and independent authority, we may expect a number of results. Perhaps the most important is the decrease in certain product differentiation advantages of established firms. Since there are some scale economies in quality assurance, grades usually make small concerns more competitive and tend to decrease seller concentration. Established firms with brand advantages are therefore generally opposed to grading proposals. From society's viewpoint, whether or not a particular good should be graded is a complex question, requiring the comparison of costs and benefits of this form of product information provision with other methods. To answer such a question, an in-depth case-by-case approach is essential.

FOR DISCUSSION

1. You are the president of B.F. Goodrich, and a serious proposal has been made for the federal grading of tires. From the perspective of your company, discuss the pros and cons of this proposal.

2. Movies are currently rated as either G, PG, R, or X. Are these grades? Explain. What is the principal industrial organization effect of these ratings?

3. As a consumer, would you want breakfast cereals to be graded? What would be the effect? Would there be more serious problems if computers were graded? What if TV sets had been graded for quality in 1947?

4. Why is it the government that usually establishes grades? Why can't this function be left to the free market? Couldn't each private testing group establish its own grading system? What would be the problems?

5. Is grading generally more useful for consumers' goods or producers' goods? Explain.

6. Do you think grading is more important in developed or less developed countries? Do you expect to find that more of Peru's or the United States' GNP is composed of graded commodities?

7. In Greece, a poor country with more foreign than domestic tourists, the government gives each hotel a quality rating and then sets the appropriate price. The national police inspect hotels, to insure that this price information is conspicuously displayed within each room. Why this governmental interference with the free market, and what are the principal economic effects? What relevance (if any) does this question have to the topic of grades?

SOURCES

Jessie V. Coles. *Standards and Labels for Consumer Goods.* New York: Ronald Press, 1949.

David Hemenway. *Industrywide Voluntary Product Standards.* Cambridge, Mass.: Ballinger, 1975.

✳ *Chapter 15*

Business Exits

During the early 1960s nearly 400,000 nonfarm enterprises closed each year. These were not mere ownership changes, but actual business exits. Every year over 8 percent of all operating firms were discontinued. For every one hundred new entrants, there were more than eighty-eight business deaths. Less than 4 percent of these closings are "failures," narrowly defined as causing losses to creditors. Most exits were to avoid future problems, to take advantage of alternative opportunities, or were due to illness, retirement, or loss of lease. (tables 15-1 and 15-2).

Business exits represent significant economic phenomena, yet receive scant attention from economists. Little statistical information on business exits has been collected, and the data that exist are relatively old. In addition, economic models are predominantly equilibrium models. The analysis is normally one of comparing different

Table 15-1. Nonfarm Business Population and Turnover: Annual Average 1960-64 (in thousands)

Year	Operating Businesses	New Enterprises	Discontinued Enterprises	Business Failures
1960-64	4750	445	394	15.2

Sources: *Survey of Current Business: Business Statistics*, 1965 ed. Office of Business Economics, pp. 10–11.
J. Cohen and S. Robbins, *The Financial Manager*, (New York: Harper & Row, 1966), p. 862.
Dun & Bradstreet, Inc., *Failure Record Through 1969*, p. 1.

Table 15-2. Motives for Liquidating Firms[a] (percent of firms)

Motive:	
Avoid Loss	48%
Lost Lease	19
Retirement, Illness	16
Alternative Opportunity	15
Dispose of at a Profit	2

[a]Based on survey replies of businessmen who liquidated concerns in the second quarter of 1946.

Source: U.S. Department of Commerce, *Survey of Current Business*, April 1947, p. 13.

static situations, with little emphasis on short-run dynamic consequences such as those of business mortality. Moreover, the microeconomic model of perfect competition assumes perfect information, universal markets, costless market transactions, and easy entry and exit, thereby eliminating the major problems associated with business exit.

This chapter briefly examines the phenomena of company deaths. It discusses the principal benefits and costs of exit, departures from the optimal amount and rate of exit, and the type of firms most likely to go out of business.

BENEFITS AND COSTS OF EXIT

Economists emphasize that in a competitive environment there are long-run benefits from business exit. Fair competition eliminates unprofitable and inefficient firms, directing resources to areas of higher productivity. Moreover, the threat of failure increases the initiative and efficiency of existing firms. Economists are thus generally concerned with the preservation of competition, not the preservation of particular competitors. It is, of course, *fair* competition that is desired, for business practices such as predatory pricing and tying agreements could cause the exit of the most efficient firms.

Even when competition is fair, however, business deaths do inflict some costs on society. For displaced workers, there may be psychic as well as job search and possibly moving costs. There are significant opportunity costs if the worker becomes unemployed. If plant and equipment are sold, there are costs associated with these transactions: finding buyers, moving machines, etc.

Some of the firm's physical capital is probably enterprise specific. For example, the interior of discontinued retail stores generally undergoes extensive remodeling when another firm takes over the lease. Part of the human capital stock is also firm specific. While much of the knowledge of workers and managers can be transferred, some cannot. Exit means that managers' knowledge of individual worker's strengths and weaknesses loses its value, as does workers' experience of how specific coworkers, managers, or machines can be expected to perform and react. Acquired team coordination and camaraderie are lost.

The discontinued firm's suppliers and customers also feel some loss. There are costs for them in finding or attracting new purchasers or new sources of supply. In the interim, they may experience short-run excess capacity, or bottlenecks may be created. Their capital stock of information is also depleted, for they had some knowledge of the intimate workings of the discontinued firm, whom to see to get things done, etc.

While these social losses from business mortality are not insignificant, it should be emphasized that they are generally transitional, or short run. Additionally, similar problems may arise even without business exit; they may be brought about merely by changes within the firm. A new leader in the company could cause many of the same minor internal and external disruptions. Most important, the enumerated costs are not caused solely by exit, but often should be attributed to the factors that led to the decision to cease operations. Keeping firms alive would not eliminate all these costs. The social value of obsolete expertise, for example, cannot be entirely restored by the simple expedient of preventing firms from going out of business.

OPTIMAL AMOUNT OF EXIT

In perfect competition, where there is perfect factor mobility and perfect markets are universal, the amount of exit is optimal from an efficiency standpoint. For example, if customers or vendors will be harmed by a particular business failure, they can contract with the firm to help keep it alive. Similarly for potentially unemployed workers. Somehow, in the model of perfect competition, such markets are not only costless to engage in, but are perfectly competitive; there is no possibility for strategic bargaining or blackmail.

In the real world, the amount and rate of exit in any market can be above or below the optimal. If competition is fair, economists tend to focus on the problems caused by too little exit. They worry about specialized and immobile resources creating barriers to exit. They stress the costs of government subsidies that keep inefficient firms alive. They cite the chronic oversupply in many American agricultural markets as having been caused by too little exit.

While too little exit may cause inefficiencies, so also can too much exit. In the real world, there are many instances where too much exit may occur. Even assuming fair competition, if a market is characterized by few sellers and high entry barriers, the demise of any firm may decrease future competition, innovation, and experimentation. The exits of Studebaker and Kaiser-Frazer from the automobile industry may have resulted in large losses for society.

Exit may become too great if fair competition becomes cutthroat. Competition, especially in high-fixed-cost industries facing cyclical swings in demand, may become so sharp as to create great instability and destroy efficient firms lacking access to liquid capital. Exit may also be socially undesirable if firms are departing because they underestimate their future prospects. There can be a net social loss when a company fails that sells a unique product that would prove popular in the future.

The general amount or speed of exit can be above the optimal simply because certain changes come too fast. Economic shocks, caused by weather, government actions, and new innovations or discoveries can sometimes create severe micro and macro problems in the short run. Technological unemployment of particular workers is a real problem, if only a transitional one.

Transition costs are often excluded from formal models, but they are clearly recognized by economists. While there is strong consensus in the profession that high tariffs are usually inimical to social welfare, there is no advocacy of immediate, severe tariff reductions. Instead the recommendation is for *gradual* reductions. Gradual reductions will decrease the short-run transition costs caused in part by the exit of some existing firms.

In the United States the dynamic costs associated with firm exit are clearly apparent in the geographic pockets of unemployment in Appalachia and in the New England textile towns. Firms were more mobile than workers, and when exit occurred, chronic underutilization of resources resulted. In these instances, resource immobility did not prevent business movement or exit, but imposed large costs on society once exit occurred.

EXIT-PRONE FIRMS

New firms and small firms are especially prone to exit. Business enterprises have high rates of infant mortality. Forty percent of new retail firms, for example, are either sold or liquidated within one year. Figure 15-1 indicates the rapid increase in life expectancy as young firms age. The high exit rate of new firms should be expected. They are competing against the best of those firms established previously. The weak and inefficient have probably gone out of business. The new firm may have difficulty establishing a foothold in the market. It may lack the product differentiation and veteran teamwork advantages of the more established concerns. It may not have as intimate a knowledge of the specific workings of the industry. For these very reasons the social cost of the discontinuance of a new firm may be less than if an older, established concern is liquidated.

Since new firms have high death rates, we expect to find high rates of exit when entry rates are high. Table 15-3 gives entry and discontinuance rates per 1000 existing firms in each of eight two-digit industries for 1952. The correlation coefficient between rates of entry and exit is .89. Similar high correlations were discovered using data from 1946 and 1949 for forty-four three-digit industries in

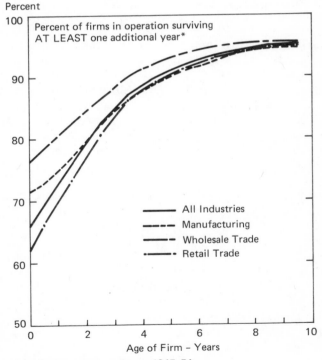

Figure 15-1. Life Expectancy of Business Firms by Age of Firm

Source: U.S. Department of Commerce, *Survey of Current Business,* December 1955, p. 15.

Table 15–3. Entry, Discontinuance and Transfer Rates[a] by Two-Digit Industry: 1952

	Entry Rate	Discontinuance Rate	Transfer Rate
All Industries	88	74	91
Mining and Quarrying	113	100	56
Contract Construction	177	115	35
Manufacturing	87	89	53
Transportation, Communication, and Other Public Utilities	132	112	48
Wholesale Trade	82	57	49
Retail Trade	77	68	137
Finance, Insurance and Real Estate	58	46	42
Service Industries	74	69	74

[a]Number of new, discontinued and transferred businesses during 1952 per 1000 firms in operation at the beginning of the year.

Source: U.S. Department of Commerce, *Survey of Current Business*, June 1954, p. 14.

manufacturing, retailing, and wholesaling. This is strong evidence indicating a close relationship between the birth and death rates of business concerns.

New firms are usually small firms. Most new entrepreneurs have very limited financial resources and enter at very small scale. We expect small firms to be more likely to experience financial difficulties, in part because they may be unable to realize full-scale economies, but mainly because they have less access to liquid capital. A short-run decrease in sales can prove fatal to the small concern. Very tiny firms are also more likely to exit, instead of being sold, since their principal asset is often the knowledge and capabilities of the owner, rather than the goodwill or going concern value of the enterprise. In such instances, the economic losses caused by exit may be very small.

The data show the high death rates of small firms. While less than 1.5 percent of "large" concerns (more than 50 employees) were discontinued in 1944, approximately 6 percent of small firms (0–3 employees) were eliminated. Such tiny companies represent over 80 percent of all business exits. (tables 15–4 and 15–5). Though evidence indicates that both youth and small size increase the likelihood of actuarial losses, the data are not sufficient to distinguish the separate effects of each of these variables on the probability of exit.

Available exit statistics give only number of enterprise exits, unweighted by sales, assets, or employees. The data are thus completely dominated by tiny firms. While the deaths of large, established firms

Table 15–4. Entry and Discontinuance Rates, by Size of Firm: 1944[a]

	Entry Rate	Discon-tinuance Rate
Total	96.2	50.6
No employees	144.3	61.5
1–3 employees	96.9	58.5
4–7 employees	49.5	32.8
8–19 employees	30.2	27.8
20–49 employees	25.2	22.5
50 or more employees	11.2	13.4

[a]Number of new and discontinued businesses during the year per 1000 firms in operation at the beginning of 1944.
Source: U.S. Department of Commerce, *Survey of Current Business*, May 1946, p. 20.

Table 15–5. Percentage of New and Discontinued Businesses by Size of Firm: 1944

	New Firms	Discon-tinued Firms
Less than 4 employees	88.9	83.9
4–7 employees	6.9	8.7
8–19 employees	2.8	4.9
20–49 employees	1.0	1.7
50 or more employees	.4	.8

Source: U.S. Department of Commerce, *Survey of Current Business*, January 1947, p. 13.

have the greatest social and economic impact, the aggregate evidence tells us principally about exits of firms with three or fewer employees.

CONCLUSION

While there is little literature or evidence concerning business exits, the economist's tendency is to emphasize the long-run benefits of business terminations, and thus to direct attention toward the possibility of insufficient exit. In this chapter, an attempt was made to enumerate some of the *costs* of exit. It was argued that given the real-world problems of unfair competition, blockaded entry, imperfect foresight, and parties affected by exit who are unable to contract with decision-makers, there can be too much as well as too little firm mortality, and exit by the wrong concerns.

The paper also examined the available statistics on business exits. The data showed that dying firms are usually young and quite small. This means that the economic problems associated with the *typical* business exit may tend to be minuscule. However, the total cost of the more than 400,000 yearly terminations could be quite large; it has never been estimated.

FOR DISCUSSION

1. Contrast exit with bankruptcy. What happened to the Penn-Central?

2. "Thirty-five percent of business terminations have been in operation less than two years. Yet only 4 percent of all failures were that young." How might you explain this fact?

3. Relate actual exits to exit barriers. Do low barriers imply high exit? High barriers, low exit? How would you go about measuring exit barriers?

4. Why are exit and entry rates correlated? If exit rates are high, indicating that many firms are not doing well, why would many new firms enter the market?

5. Do you think the actual number of firms exiting increased or decreased during the Great Depression? Think carefully and explain your answer.

6. Do you expect exit rates to be higher or lower in the United States or the USSR? Higher or lower in Sweden? Haiti?

7. Do economists tend to favor the subsidization of a company like Lockheed? What are the economic costs of Lockheed's going out of business? Would this be more or less than if one hundred retail firms, each with 1 percent of Lockheed's sales closed throughout the country?

8. Table 15-3 indicates that manufacturing has a higher rate of exit than retail trade. Is this what you might expect? How would you explain this fact?

9. Relate exits to the product life cycle. Are actual exits likely to increase or decrease as the industry matures? What do you expect to happen to exit barriers?

10. How can the costs of dynamic change be measured? Do exits give a good indication of the true costs?

11. Describe the kind of statistics on business exits it would be useful to collect. Explain how and why they would be useful.

SOURCES

William L. Crum. *The Age Structure of the Corporate System*, Berkeley: University of California Press, 1953.

Warren W. Etcheson. *A Study of Business Terminations*, Seattle: Business Research Bureau, University of Washington, 1962.

Edwin Mansfield. "Entry, Gibrat's Law, Innovation, and the Growth of Firms." *American Economic Review* 52 (December 1962).

Matityahu Marcus. "Firms' Exit Rates and Their Determinants." *Journal of Industrial Economics* 16(November 1967).

Alfred R. Oxenfeldt. *New Firms and Free Enterprise*. Washington, D.C.: American Council on Public Affairs, 1943.

H.O. Stekler. *Profitability and Size of Firm*. Berkeley: Institute of Business and Economic Research, University of California, 1963.

Chapter 16

The Ice Trust

INTRODUCTION

The first great American merger wave had a dramatic effect on the structure of U.S. industry. This early merger movement, culminating in the flurry of consolidations between 1898 and 1902, left an imprint on the American economy that seventy-five years has not erased. It was during these years that the pattern of concentration characteristic of American business formed and matured.[1] During these four years, 236 important industrial consolidations occurred, with total capital of $6.1 billion.[2] By 1904 the trusts controlled fully 40 percent of the manufacturing capital of the country.[3] It was during this period that U.S. Steel was formed, U.S. Rubber, the Tobacco Trust, American Can, U.S. Gypsum, General Electric, International Nickel, International Paper, Allis-Chalmers, United Shoe, United Fruit, Standard Sanitary, National Lead, Pullman Company, National Biscuit Company, the Sugar Trust, International Salt, Western Union, etc. Also during this period, a wide variety of less important trusts emerged, including those in bicycles, caramels, grass twine, hominies, chewing gum, buttons, and ice.[4]

This is the story of one of the most fascinating of the lesser trusts, the ice trust, which briefly but spectacularly succeeded in gaining monopoly control over the New York City ice supply. It is the story of Charles W. Morse, tycoon and robber baron, founder and president of the American Ice Company, who ruthlessly ordered prices raised and service cut upon securing his monopoly position. And it is the story of the ensuing public outcry, combined with natural competitive forces, which dethroned the ice trust and quickly sent prices tumbling to pretrust levels.

THE AMERICAN ICE COMPANY

At the turn of the century, the residents of New York City received most of their ice from natural sources, principally cuttings from the Hudson and the Penobscot and Kennebec rivers in Maine. Though the supply of manufactured ice was rapidly increasing in both absolute and relative terms, artificial ice still accounted for less than 15 percent of the city's annual four-million-ton consumption.[5] The reliance upon natural ice resulted in pronounced fluctuations in prices and profits depending upon the vagaries of the climate. Warm winters decreased the supply of ice and increased the cost of harvesting.[6] Warm winters also increased the demand, as did hot summers. The warm weather in 1905–1906, for example, raised the winter sales in New York City 50 percent over the previous winter.[7] The effect of the warm weather in 1905–1906 and 1912–1913 is shown clearly in the profits of the American Ice Company. In the former period, net profits jumped from $487,000 in 1904–1905 to over $2 million, falling back to $185,000 the next year. And from $369,000 in 1911–12, annual profits climbed the following year to $1,600,000, dropping to $400,000 in 1913–14.[8]

The American Ice Company was the "ice trust," incorporated in 1899 with Charles W. Morse as president. An independent Maine ice operator, Morse, during the warm New York winter of 1890, had been able to acquire control of the starved-for-ice New York City and Consumers' Ice companies. In 1895 these and other small companies were incorporated into the new Consolidated Ice Company, whose stated objectives were to regulate prices, restrict the amount harvested, and hold down competition.[9] The important Knickerbocker Ice Companies of New York and New Jersey soon joined the alliance.[10] Consolidated thus already had substantial control over the New York market at the time of the formation of the American Ice Company.

Incorporated under the friendly laws of New Jersey, the American Ice Company formally merged Consolidated, Knickerbocker of Maine, and a goodly number of smaller manufacturers and distributors. The combination possessed extensive plants for the housing of ice on the Penobscot, Kennebec, Schuylkill, Susquehanna, and Hudson rivers, Rockland Lake, Croton Lake, and many New Jersey lakes. It also controlled a number of plants for manufacturing artificial ice in New York City, Philadelphia, Camden, Atlantic City, Baltimore, and Washington, D.C., and owned dock facilities and real esate in virtually all of these cities. Moody's listed the number of plants acquired as "about 40," and the proportion of the industry controlled locally as 80 percent.[11]

ELIMINATING COMPETITION

Attaining and, especially, maintaining a monopoly position in ice was not an easy proposition. Ice is a largely homogeneous product, and neither a great deal of capital nor technical expertise was required to enter the natural, or even the artificial, ice business.[12] Not only were entry barriers low, but the market was reasonably large and growing. Total U.S. consumption of ice more than tripled between 1880 and 1914.[13]

The ice trust engaged in a variety of practices designed to limit competition. One device was the restrictive convenant. Managers of acquired companies were required to sign agreements prohibiting them from engaging in the ice business for a period of ten years. These restrictive covenants seem to have been of some importance. In 1902 *Ice and Refrigeration*, a trade journal, reported that the American Ice Company had obtained a permanent injunction from the Supreme Court restraining certain of the exdealers from engaging in the retail ice trade.[15] In late 1909 these covenants were attacked under the New York antitrust statute, but this specific charge was dropped since most of the contracts had expired or were shortly to expire.[16]

The ice trust had other more ruthless ways of crushing competition. One story reported in the *Times* told of the persecution of independent ice dealer W.A. Wynne. The steamer *Norwich* twice smashed all the ice in front of his place of business. She was equipped for this very purpose.[17]

The ice trust's alliance with the Tammany city government seems to have played a key role in eliminating stubborn competitors. One ice-dealer, Richard Foster, paid over $2000 a year to the city for his docking privilege. After he refused to sell to Morse, this privilege was revoked and his ice bridge was cut four times by the Dock Department on the excuse that it obstructed snow dumping. When it was learned that such treatment was to be officially inquired into, the harassment stopped.[18] Other ice-dealers were told to get out of their berths by the Dock Department, because the spots were needed for something else. They left, only to watch the ice trust move into the vacated berths.[19]

A further method by which the trust attempted to limit competition was by its strict resale rules to its large (lower-price) customers. Restaurants, ice-cream saloons, liquor dealers, all were told that if they sold so much as a pound of ice, even in an emergency, in the case of a contract it would be abrogated, and in the case of a cash customer, he would be left out in the cold.[21]

THE PRICE HIKE

In April 1900, a year after its formation, the ice trust arbitrarily doubled its price. For large customers, prices rose from 15¢ to 25¢/100 lb., or $5/ton. The small consumer was more severely hurt. Here prices rose from 25¢ to 60¢/100 lb., with hints of further advances to come. In addition, households were informed that deliveries would be made only thrice a week, instead of daily. This was a special hardship since few refrigerators in private homes could hold a two-day supply of ice. The trust also eliminated the 5¢ and 10¢ chunk, the size most convenient for the poor.[22] (This was at a time when the *Times* cost a penny, the *Sunday Times*, 3¢.)

There appears to have been no cost justification for the doubling of prices. While the trust blamed the shortness of supply, *Ice and Refrigeration* refuted the cry of famine. This independent Chicago publication stated: "The much-talked of ice famine apparently exists only in the minds of would-be speculators."[23] The Hudson River crop was only slightly less than normal, and since the previous year's crop had been record-breaking (4.3 million tons, or greater than the total New York City ice consumption), there was much left over. Combined with the Maine crop and the manufactured product, there was little shortage in 1900.[24]

Additional evidence attesting to the administered nature of the price rise comes from intercity comparisons. No city had as high a price as New York. In areas where competition existed, prices were little different from previous years. In Buffalo, Boston, Albany, and Bangor, there were no advances. Only in cities like New York and Philadelphia, where the ice trust was strong, did prices increase.[25]

The *Times* claimed that the trust had tried to limit the crop by cutting only fourteen- and twelve-inch ice, whereas ten-inch ice was usually cut, and by leaving much ice unharvested. The trust seems not to have permanently reduced the 1900 supply, however, for when prices returned to their former levels, as they shortly did, no ice shortage occurred in New York City.[26]

PUBLIC OUTCRY

The Tammany Connection

Public outcry against the price hike was strong and clamorous and had its effect. The quickness of the trust's retreat was probably caused by the immense public resentment over the price hike, especially when combined with the subsequent exposure of the trust's shady dealings. The trust did not drop its prices because of a sudden reawakening to its social responsibilities. Instead, the quickness of the price reduction is more explicable in terms of crude "jawboning," with the bludgeon of state antitrust action clearly visible. But the responsibility lies with an aroused press and citizenry, rather than with an alert and concerned government. Indeed, an important portion of the local government had already embraced the trust.

The public first learned of a Tammany-ice-trust connection in the spring of 1899. On the day that "Boss" Richard Croker's personal representative, John F. Carroll, was to testify before the State Legislative Investigating Committee (the Mazet Committee) a newspaper ran a story charging that Carroll and others were American Ice Company stockholders. When questioned about it, Carroll refused to testify. "It is a personal matter," he said. "I decline to answer it." Boss Croker then took the stand and also initially declined to respond. It was disclosed, however, that Croker had once owned stock, but no longer did. "I turned it over to another person." Q: "Who is that?" A: "In my family, my wife." Croker's wife, it was discovered, owned at least 150 shares, then worth some $40 a share. The family further owned substantial holdings of the Knickerbocker Ice Company of Philadelphia, which had joined the trust.[27] A year later, less than a month after the famed price hike, the mayor of New York, Robert A. Van Wyck, went on a pleasure trip to Maine, accompanied by John Carroll, both as guests of Charles W. Morse, head of the ice trust.[28] Editorialized the *Times*, this excursion "cannot escape remark."[29]

Following on the heels of the price advance, a paper's (and people's) crusade began. The *Times* was silent for three weeks, but then ran strong editorials against the "hoggish monopoly."[30] The *New York Evening Post* ran articles showing that municipal ice plants could be constructed to produce ice for delivery at 10¢/100 lb.[31] But the most important action was taken by the *New York Journal*, leading newspaper of the Democratic party. It was the *Journal* that strongly asserted that the Tammany Democratic machine held large blocks of ice trust stock, and it was at the instigation of Randolph Hearst himself that the attorney general of New York began an investigation of the company. None of the criminal or civil cases initially brought against the American Ice Company ever amounted to anything, but the exposed facts had a sensational effect.[32]

In June of 1900 an official stockholders list was made public. Mayor Robert Van Wyck was shown to hold 2660 shares of preferred stock and 3325 shares of common stock, par value at $100, but selling at $48 in April and falling fast to a record low of $28 on the day after this announcement. It was further disclosed that Morse had let Van Wyck have the stock at "bed-rock price" (half of par) and, in effect, lent him the money with which to buy it![33] (Throughout this trying period there were continual, but false, rumors of the mayor's imminent retirement.)[34]

Another prominent name on the list was the mayor's brother, former judge Augustus Van Wyck, who had unsuccessfully opposed Theodore Roosevelt for governor of New York in 1898, and had been mentioned as a possible vice-presidential candidate. It is of interest that Augustus had been touted as the eloquent champion of the movement against the trusts. Wrote the *Independent:* "His utterances against Trust monopolies and exactions are among the most valued campaign documents of his party."[35] The *Independent* felt that the ice scandal might prevent Augustus from being a delegate-at-large at the next convention, though they pointed out that Republican Thurston of Nebraska had recently been elected delegate-at-large upon the platform of denouncing the trusts at the same time that he was defending Standard Oil in Court.[36]

Also on the stockholder's list were John Carroll, Boss Crocker's vicegerent, as well as numerous judges and dock commissioners Cram and Murphy. These two officials possessed the principal power to grant or refuse docking facilities to any (ice) firm in New York City. It is estimated that over 50 percent of the property suitable for docking in Manhattan was public, or under their control. While Cram had sold his 100 shares of stock, Murphy still possessed his 200, worth close to $10,000 in April of 1900.[37]

The scandal had its effect on Tammany. The *Independent* reported that Boss Croker and Carroll turned the Tammany delegation to Bryan, and that out-of-city Democrats in New York were preparing to denounce the Ice Company in the coming state convention.[38] At that convention, Tammany did not dare assert itself.[39] In the city the *Times* ran headlines declaring: "Ice Trust's Action Alarms Tammany Men; Rank and File Fear the Effect on Public Sentiment."[40] The Van Wyck brothers were obviously in disfavor.

At the subsequent mayoral election the Tammany candidate was defeated by a "reform mayor," elected by the fusion of all other parties. Interestingly the major issue was not the ice scandal, but the police scandal![41]

The response of the public to the trust's price hike and the Tammany involvement seems to have been substantial. Continually the *Times* reported that the trust "is talked of everywhere, from the slums to the clubs, in Wall Street, and on street cars. Plans to thwart the combine are considered by the most lowly as well as by the most intelligent."[42] And, in general, the *Times* concluded, the trust is "now loathed by the community."[43]

The Nature of the Product

The public outcry against the trust was largely due to the particular nature of the product. Ice was more of a necessity in 1900 than a luxury. It was virtually essential for the preservation of foods, and doctors had already documented the relationship between infant mortality and drastic heat or ice shortages when it was difficult for the poor to preserve milk. The poor spent a noticeable part of their income in purchasing ice, a product often bought daily, at a price clearly visible. Further, ice seems to have been thought of not only as a vital necessity, but also something of a gift from nature, or a "free good." Wrote the *Times:* "To corner ice is very much like cornering air and water."[45]

It appears quite important that the product monopolized was ice. Wrote the *Outlook;*

> Had Tammany been prime movers in the organization of the wire and steel trust, their constituents would not have cared, for stock-jobbing operations do not really concern them, and the price of wire fences, or even wire nails, is to them a matter of supreme indifference. Had they been prominent in the management of the oil trust, they might incur a slight unpopularity, but even the price of oil concerns but little the voters of a great city to whom gas is the cheaper illuminant. But when the leaders of Tammany Hall became connected with the ice trust, and that trust advanced prices 100%, the wrath of the whole East Side was aroused against the hypocrisy as well as the extortion of its professed defenders.[46]

The sensitivity of the public to substantial increases in the price of ice is amply demonstrated by the outrage during the real shortages in 1906 and 1913. Though high prices during these years were prompted principally by demand and supply conditions (these were very warm winters), antitrust action was either brought or seriously considered in New York, Philadelphia, Washington, D.C., Boston,

Baltimore, and Toledo. Little came of these actions save in Toledo, where a number of businessmen served thirty-seven days in jail.[47] Between 1906 and 1913 there was a great deal of careful attention given to the possibility of government-owned ice plants. In 1910 the mayor of Schenectady was elected partly on his program for "ice-at-cost." The shortage in 1913 prompted the city of New York to finance the Wentworth Report on municipal ice plants. While quite favorable to the construction of municipal plants, the report indicated that there was then only one in existence in the United States, in Weatherford, Okalahoma![48] With the gradual replacement of manufactured for natural ice, the fluctuations in the supply and price of ice decreased, as did the public clamor for some sort of governmental action.

The Hoggish Monopoly

The clamor raised against the ice trust in 1900 was due not to the fact that it possessed some degree of monopoly power, but that it had used that power so arrogantly and brutally. The *Times*, which went out of its way to explain that it was only averse to "bad" trusts, attacked this "hoggish monopoly" that was "holding up" the community.[49] *Gunton's Magazine* (like the *Times*, and most economists of the day) was not against trusts in general, but was violently opposed to this "bungling burglar" that would bring discredit to its class. "The people," said *Gunton's*, "can be fooled for a while if the fooling is skillfully done, but when not it is bunglingly performed."[50]

The people obviously were not fooled, and their outcry helped secure the trust's quick defeat. Six weeks after the initial price hike, the trust agreed to sell 5¢ pieces, but "would make no further concessions." The *Times* strongly denounced this "Public be Damned" attitude.[51] Two weeks later, following the official publication of the Tammany Ice Holdings, prices were quietly slashed from 60¢ to 40¢/100 lbs., which the *Times* editors called "a famous victory."[52] Within the week, prices were 25¢ for most sectors of the city, as the Trust met the price of any independent selling below the 40¢ rate.

In late June the *Times* ran an article under "Ice Plenty and Cheap" (prices still varied from 25¢ to 50¢) which contained this picturesque description of the small ice market:

> Ice was in evidence everywhere on the crowded east side streets. Each block had from one to half a dozen vendors on it, some with huge stores or several tons just from the bridges; others pushed carts which started out with a cake of ice and made journey after journey to the base of supplies as the vendors sold out. Everybody seemed to be buying ice. On stoops

and in hallways were women with broods of children and a pitcher of ice-water which was drunk as if it was nectar. Housewives with pans and dishes and cloths left their domestic work to get a chunk of the gelid necessary for 5 or 10¢, and each cart or wagon had its following of children who scrambled for small ice refuse and greedily crushed it.[53]

ENTRY

By November the ice market was glutted.[54] The major cause for the surplus was, as might be expected, the entry of new firms lured by the trust's high prices and profits. Earlier that spring, when prices were high, the *Times* reported the formation of the Empire Ice Co., with a manufacturing ice capacity of 600 tons/day, and which did "not believe in the exorbitant price which the Trust is asking."[55] The Green Island Ice Co. began building a wharf on Sedgwick Street and was expecting to undersell the trust during the summer.[56] The Bronx Consumers Ice Co. was incorporated with capital of $100,000, and business purchasers of ice in Brooklyn were seriously considering forming their own "Anti-Trust Ice Company."[57]

The "impetuous rush to form new companies"[58] during "prosperous" times—the perennial fear of the ice industry—seems largely responsible for the oversupply in late 1900. That overentry, or overoptimism of the entrants, was a problem is attested to by company failures large enough to be reported in the *Times*. In the spring of 1901, for example, the Manhattan Ice Company, formed the previous June, employing forty men and serving two thousand customers, toppled.[59] Two years later the People's Co-Op Ice Company, formed in August 1900, with a capital stock of over $1 million, also went under.[60] Fortunately for the industry, while entry was relatively easy, so apparently, was exit.

The rapid entry into the ice industry during the period of high trust prices undoubtedly meant that the public's "famous victory" only speeded the inevitable. For all its ruthlessness, the trust was unable to raise entry barriers to a degree sufficient to allow a large monopoly profit. Its attempt to realize that profit brought a rash of new competitors, decreasing the price and eroding the trust's market position. As the *Times* predicted in the spring of 1900: "It may turn out that the hoggish monopoly has outwitted itself by its hoggishness."[61] "(I)ts recklessness has endangered the health, if it has not insured the death, of the goose relied on to lay the golden eggs."[62]

Was the action of the trust's management in raising prices and inviting entry and condemnation really so irrational? For the long-term health and viability of the American Ice Co., the move was clearly unfortunate. The troubles of the company "really date to the outburst of public condemnation and disfavor in 1900."[63] The stock, selling at $49 in the spring of 1900, fell to $4 3/4 in 1903 during the general stock market decline.[64] Reported profits dropped from close to a million dollars in 1900, to $650,000 in 1901, to a *deficit* of $162,000 in 1902.[65] The American Ice Company was clearly in dire straits. *Ice and Refrigeration* reported in the spring of 1903: "If a second cool summer with limited demand for ice should come, no holding company scheme could save the big 'ice trust' from dissolution."[66]

CHARLES W. MORSE

While the company and common owners of the stock were severely hurt by the ice trust's attempted "hold-up" of the community, the president of the corporation certainly was not. Though an identity of interests between the owners and controllers of a corporation is often assumed, in this case, what was good for Charles W. Morse was not very good for the American Ice Company. While even Mayor Van Wyck lost money [67] on this weirdly overcapitalized venture (most of the $60 million capitalization was pure "water"), Charlie Morse is reported to have withdrawn from the corporation in 1901 with over $12 million![68]

Since Morse played such a crucial role in the formation and actions of the ice trust, it is of interest to digress a bit and briefly examine his colorful and checkered career. Morse was far more of a promoter, speculator, and financial manipulator than he was a conservative or conventional businessman. After his reign as "Ice King" at the turn of the century, he turned more intensively to shipping and banking. By 1907, through a series of billiant operations, he managed to achieve something close to a monopoly of coastwise shipping from Bangor to Galveston, and became known as "the Admiral of the Atlantic." The panic of 1907, however, found the Heinze-Morse banks at the storm center; an investigation resulted in Morse's indictment and conviction for false entries and the misapplication of funds.[69]

While Morse argued that "there is no one in Wall Street who is not daily doing as I have done,"[70] this "fat, squatty little man" with the "masterful inquiring eyes" was sentenced to a fifteen-year term in the Atlanta penitentiary. Every exertion by Morse's friends and relatives to secure a pardon or commutation of sentence from President Taft proved unavailing. Finally, in 1912 Harry Daugherty, later attorney general in the Harding cabinet, contracted with Morse for a retainer of five thousand dollars, and promise of an additional twenty-five thousand in case of success, to secure his release. A commission of doctors examined Morse and reported he was suffering from Bright's disease, and could not last the year. Taft reluctantly signed a pardon. However, Daugherty's fee remained unpaid, and the attorney-general's office received information that before his examination, Morse had drunk a combination of soapsuds and chemicals calculated to produce the desired temporary effects. President Taft later charged he had been deluded in the whole affair, adding that the case "shakes one's faith in expert examination."[71]

In 1916 Morse again made news with a grandiose scheme for organizing an American transoceanic shipping combination. This assumed reality with the formation of a holding company, the United States Shipping Company. The company prospered during the war, but in the subsequent "war frauds" investigation Morse was again indicted. Before that case could be brought, he was further indicted on the charge of using the mails to defraud potential investors. Before this "mail frauds" case was complete, Morse was adjudged too ill to stand trial. He was placed under guardianship, declared too incompetent to handle his own affairs, and died some seven years later in his home town of Bath, Maine at the age of seventy-six.[72]

THE AMERICAN ICE COMPANY
AFTER 1903

Morse and his immediate successor seemingly attempted to milk the corporation dry before the crisis of 1903 and the stockholder's revolt. Before that corporate emergency, the common public stockholder had been virtually powerless to take any action. He was unable to discover the actual ownership of the company (it took a court order to get the official listing during the 1900 Tammany-trust investigation), or the actual control (because of the numerous dummy directorates), or even the earnings of the trust. The *Times*, for example, gave this seemingly tongue-in-cheek account of the 1902 stockholders meeting: "It was understood beforehand that the officers of the company would violate the precedent of the past annual meetings and submit a statement of the actual earnings of the company. The corporation regularly pays 6% annual dividend on preferred stock, 4% on common. . . . No precedents were violated however."[73]

The stockholders' meeting in 1903 was a very lively affair. The American Ice Company had just announced a deficit for the preced-

ing year, and stock prices had broken to $4 3/4. A number of promi-
nent stockholders charged, among other things, that the officers of
the trust had declared dividends when there were no earnings, had
paid unnecessarily liberal commissions for the sale of bonds, had purchased the Knickerbocker Steam Towage Co. at an excessive price
benefiting a few insiders in the trust's management, and had used the
power of the trust to enhance their own holding in an independent
ice company. It was from the pressure of these minority stockholders that an investigating committee, albeit a conservative one,
was eventually formed to examine the charges and generally report
on the condition of the company.[74]

The report of the stockholders investigating committee helped to
document the extent of the trust's overcapitalization and corporate
mismanagement. While capitalization had been reduced from $60
to $40 million, the committee reported that the company's real
property was worth only $15 million, and there was "nothing
between this and the preferred stock." The $25 million in common
stock, in other words, represented pure "good will."[75] (Note the
irony.) The financial difficulties of the company were attributed
largely to the payment of unearned dividends. The milking of the
corporation was further attested to by the fact that 1903 marked
the "first time in several years that the company made liberal expenditures" to improve its real estate.[76] Many of the other charges
against the trust were seemingly not examined. Morse undoubtedly
made things difficult by generally keeping no books and "destroying all records of deals soon after they were closed."[77]

In 1904, Wesley Oler took over as president of the American Ice
Company. Oler was a friend of Morse and a member of the original
trust, but he was a sound businessman and stayed with the company
for many years, making it a profitable, if not a growing, concern.
Oler died in 1927, two years before the corporation reached its all-
time peak sales of $20.8 million, and all-time peak profits of $3.4
million. The firm was finally absorbed around 1960, with its sales
still in the $15-18 million range.[78]

In 1905, Oler again reduced the company's capitalization, but
book assets still remained largely "good will account, water rights,
and patent rights." These become of less and less value as the natural
ice properties were discarded and displaced by manufacturing plants.
By the early twenties, virtually all of the business of the American
Ice Company was in manufactured ice. Yet it was well into the
Depression before all the natural ice properties were written off.[79]

The American Ice Company made numerous attempts to diversify,
into the distribution of coal and wood, the repair of wagons, the dis-

tillation of water, etc., but the sale of ice continued to provide the vast majority of its revenues into the late twenties and thirties, when electric refrigeration became more common. In 1941 the American Ice Company was still the second largest distributor of manufactured ice in the country, with 50 percent of its $12 million gross sales coming from ice, the rest from fuel oil and laundry services.[80] Of interest in the diversification attempts of the company was the change in its charter made in 1907 to allow it to "acquire, own, equip, operate, and dispose of steamships."[81] This scheme, however, seems to have been quickly dropped when the "Admiral of the Atlantic" was indicted and sent to prison.

Probably the most intriguing episode of the Oler regime occurred in 1906 when a true ice shortage hit New York City, which still relied on the American Ice Company for about half its ice.[82] The general shortage was so acute that for a while, in September, the company was essentially without ice as its fully laden Maine schooners were fogbound in the Atlantic.[83] Prices, of course, were high that year, and the trust made handsome profits, but the company had obviously learned from its 1900 experience. In March, the trust announced its intent "to do everything possible to prevent an increase in public indignation."[84] And in June the trust declared that, no matter what, families would not have to pay more than 40¢/100 lbs. If prices were to increase, the burden would be on hotels, stores, and other large customers. Further, the 10¢ piece (25 lbs.) would remain on sale.[85]

CONCLUSION

Like many turn-of-the-century trusts, the American Ice Company succeeded in gaining monopoly control over the market. The ice trust, however, had more problems than most in maintaining that position, in some part due to the high visibility and essential nature of the product, but primarily because of the easy entry into the industry. When the trust did abuse its limited economic power, raising prices and decreasing the services associated with the product, these actions proved quite detrimental to its own long-term welfare. (The long-term welfare of the corporation, however, was of no great concern to its early president, whose primary interest was in securing his own short-run profit.) Three years after its formation, the American Ice Company was on the brink of bankruptcy.

While the American Ice Company was only one of the many monopolies formed at the turn of the century, the ice trust was nevertheless a historical phenomenon of some singularity. Among other things, the disclosure of the Tammany-trust connection caused political ripples, and the newspaper crusade demonstrated the effectiveness of public outrage, especially when coupled with strong underlying economic forces. Basically, however, the year of the ice trust provided a unique, if not very plesant, experience for many residents of New York City—and a lot of money for Charles W. Morse.

FOR DISCUSSION

1. What really was the economic effect of the public outcry against the ice trust? What would have heppened had there been none?

2. Does the nature of the product actually affect whether or not the government will interfere in a market? Is the public more likely to demand the regulation of consumer goods industries? Of conspicuous industries? Cite some examples.

3. Economists generally assume that corporations try to maximize profits. Is this a fruitful assumption? A valid one? Is it more or less likely to be accurate for small or large companies?

4. Can you name the president of IBM, or GM or GE or Exxon? Are businessmen today less conspicuous than they were in 1900? Less identifiable with a specific company? Explain. What is the economic effect, if any?

5. What are the arguments for and against national (vs. state) incorporation laws? What is the purpose of having corporate charters?

6. Does it ever make sense for a profit-maximizing monopolist to price so high as to attract entry? Explain.

7. Should the government worry about horizontal mergers in industries with low entry barriers? Why or why not?

NOTES TO CHAPTER 16

1. J.W. Markham, "Survey of the Evidence and Findings on Mergers," in National Bureau of Economic Research publication, *Business Concentration and Price Policy*, 1952, pp. 141–82.

2. John Moody, *The Truth about Trusts*, 1904.

3. Henry Seager and Charles Gulick, Jr. *Trust and Corporation Problems* (New York: Arno, 1929), p. 61.

4. Moody.

5. *New York Times*, 2 February 1906.

6. "Some Facts on Present Conditions in the Ice Trade," *Ice and Refrigeration* (July 1906), p. 16.

7. *New York Times*, 2 March 1906.

8. John Moody, *Railroad and Corporate Securities*, annual, 1905-1915.

9. *New York Times*, 6 May 1900.

10. Richard O. Cummings, *The American Ice Harvests* (Berkeley, University of California Press, 1949), p. 87.

11. Moody, pp. 227-28.

12. As late as 1913, Milwaukee officials estimated the cost of an efficient municipal ice plant at $150,000. Jeanie Wells Wentworth, *A Report on Municipal and Government Ice Plants in the United States and Other Countries* (New York: M.B. Brown, 1913), pp. 60-62.

13. Oscar Edward Anderson, Jr., *Refrigeration in America* (Princeton: Princeton University Press, 1953), p. 114.

14. *New York Times*, 6 May 1900.

15. "Ice Trade Notes," *Ice and Refrigeration*, February 1902, p. 54.

16. "Ice Trade Notes," *Ice and Refrigeration*, November 1909, p. 191.

17. *New York Times*, 9 May 1900.

18. Ibid., 4 May 1900. 5/4(7:3).

19. Ibid., 6 May 1900. 5/6(18:5).

20. Ibid.

21. *New York Times*, 6 March 1900.

22. Ibid., 26 March, 5 May, 6 June 1900.

23. Ibid., 6 June 1900.

24. *Ice and Refrigeration*, August 1901, p. 46.

25. Ibid., 7 May 1900.

26. Ibid., 6 May, 2 June 1900.

27. Ibid., 15 April 1899.

28. Ibid., 4 May 1900.

29. Ibid., 5 May 1900.

30. Ibid., 26 March, 7 May, 8 May 1900.

31. "Ice Trust Exactions," *The Outlook*, 19 May 1900, p. 144.

32. "Ice and Politics," *The Independent*, 31 May 1900, p. 1331; Owen Wilson, "Admiral of the Atlantic Coast," *Worlds Work*, April 1907.

33. *New York Times*, 3 June, 10 June 1900.

34. Ibid., 12 June, 1900.

35. "Ice and Politics," *The Independent*, 31 May 1900, p. 1331.

36. Ibid.

37. *New York Times*, 10 June 1900.

38. "Ice and Politics," *The Independent*, 31 May 1900, p. 1332.

39. "Ice Trust in Politics," *The Outlook*, 16 June 1900.

40. *New York Times*, 8 May 1900.

41. "Robert A. Van Wyck," *Dictionary of American Biography* (New York: Charles Scribner's Sons, 1934).

42. *New York Times*, 6 May 1900.

43. Ibid., 26 April, 1900.

44. Ibid., 29 May 1900.

45. Ibid., 20 April 1900.

46. "New York's Ice Trust," *The Outlook*, 9 June 1900, p. 328.

47. *New York Times*, 26 June, 29 June, 4 July, 7 July, 13 July, 1906; "Ice Trade Notes," *Ice and Refrigeration*, April 1908, p. 209.

48. Jeanie Wentworth, *A Report on Municipal and Government Ice Plants*, p. 66. The call for municipal plants in 1900 was cooled by the Tammany-trust connections.

49. *New York Times*, 26 April 1900.

50. "Ice Trust Outrage," *Gunton's Magazine*, June 1900, pp. 515–19.

51. *New York Times*, 16 May, 20 May 1900.

52. Ibid., 8 June 1900.

53. Ibid., 29 June 1900.

54. Ibid., 15 November, 18 November 1900.

55. Ibid., 9 May 1900.

56. Ibid.

57. *New York Times*, 10 May 1900.

58. "Ice Trade Notes," *Ice and Refrigeration*, August 1906, p. 59.

59. *New York Times*, 23 April 1901.

60. Ibid., 23 October 1903.

61. Ibid., 26 April 1900.

62. Ibid., 7 May 1900.

63. American Ice Company Stockholders Committee Report, 1903, quoted in Moody's *Manual of Industrial and Miscellaneous Securities*, 1904.

64. *Wall Street Journal*, 24 October 1903, quoted in Moody, *Truth about Trusts*, p. 479.

65. Moody, *Truth about Trusts*, p. 227.

66. "Ice Trade Notes," *Ice and Refrigeration*, May 1903, p. 197.

67. The mayor sold all his stock in June 1900 at a slight loss (*New York Times*, 10 November 1900).

68. See Wilson, "Admiral of the Atlantic"; also "Water Still Freezes," *Fortune*, May 1933.

69. "Charles W. Morse," *Dictionary of American Biography*, 1934.

70. Current Literature, February 1910, p. 153, quoted in *Dictionary of American Biography*.

71. New York Times, 16 November 1913, quoted in *Dictionary of American Biography*.

72. "Morse," *Dictionary of American Biography*.

73. *New York Times*, 12 March 1902.

74. *New York Times*, 11 March, 29 April 1903; "Ice Trade Notes," *Ice and Refrigeration*, April 1903, p. 163.

75. "Ice Trade Notes," *Ice and Refrigeration*, January 1904, p. 59.

76. Ibid.; *New York Times*, 21 November 1903.

77. John E. MacDonald tried to sue Morse for $200,000 in 1904. The above is from Morse's testimony. See *New York Times*, 25 October 1904; "Ice Trade Notes," *Ice and Refrigeration*, November 1904, p. 188.

78. Moody's, and then Poor's *Manuals of Corporate Securities:* 1900–1960.

79. Moody's *Manual of Railroad and Corporate Securities:* 1904, 1905, 1912, 1924. "Water Still Freezes," *Fortune*, May 1933.

80. Moody's (Poor's), 1941.
81. Ibid., 1907.
82. *New York Times*, 24 September 1906.
83. Ibid., 23 September 1906.
84. Ibid., 14 March 1906.
85. Ibid., 10 June 1906.

❋ *Part V*

The Economic Approach

INTRODUCTION

In a fundamental sense, microeconomic theory is a theory of rational behavior. It describes how individuals should act in order to maximize their utility, and typically assumes that all individuals will try to act in this manner. In this sense, alcoholics, criminals, and saints are treated alike. The only distinction among them is that they have differing preferences and desires.

The assumption of rationality is basic to the analysis employed in this part. Chapter 17 concerns both alcoholics and criminals. It deals specifically with skid row areas and tries to explain the crime that exists in these slums. How skid rows develop is also discussed, and the public-policy option of skid row dispersal is analyzed.

In a lighter vein, Chapter 18 takes a look at the Bible from an economic perspective. The focus is upon the notion of scarcity, which is discussed with respect to the story of the creation and the teachings of Jesus. Both chapters in this section are designed to show how an economist might approach a number of unusual topics, and to further illustrate the way economists think.

Chapter 17

Skid Row

At the bottom of the modern urban social structure lies skid row.[a] Skid row is a slum, a highly deteriorated, mixed commercial and residential area inhabited by disaffiliated or "homeless" men. The skid row area is characterized by substandard hotels and rooming houses, cheap saloons and restaurants, religious missions and other institutions that provide services for the indigent male community.

HISTORY

While homeless men—beggars, refugees, outlaws, religious mendicants, migratory workers, etc.—have been around for hundreds of years, urban skid row appeared only about a century ago. In the United States, three great social upheavals—the Civil War, massive European immigration, and the depression of the 1870s—vastly increased the number of homeless men stationed in the growing urban environment. It was during this period that specialized urban areas emerged to service the large vagrant population.[1]

By the turn of the century, skid row areas were visible in almost all major American cities and were expanding rapidly. Demand for casual labor was high, for men were needed to clear forests, build railroads, and harvest crops. Skid row served as an employment center for the unskilled laborer who was willing to travel and work on

---

[a]The term *skid row* derives from Seattle's Skid Road, a trail down which logs were skidded to the saw mills on Puget Sound. Loggers built their shacks along this track, and bars, flophouses, and brothels soon followed.

temporary jobs for low wages. Such employment opportunities in the early twentieth century made skid row populations both highly mobile and seasonally variable.

In 1915, population on Chicago's skid row is estimated to have been on the order of 50,000, expanding in winter and shrinking during summer working months. Manhattten's Bowery housed a population of similar size.[2] Both these and other skid row areas were quickly depleted by the entrance of the United States into World War I. The war increased the supply of stable, better-paying jobs and decreased the size of the skid row community.

When the war ended, skid row was rapidly repopulated. As the Civil War veterans had once helped to establish skid rows, so the returning veterans of World War I helped to reoccupy them. There was little change in the population of skid row during the 1920s. Then came the Great Depression, swelling the number of homeless, poor, and unemployed. Skid Row reached its peak size during this period, as many men were forced or drawn there by the cheap living conditions and relative ease of obtaining relief.

During World War II, skid row population again diminished drastically. The New York City municipal lodging house, for example, which housed some 19,000 per day in 1935, averaged only 550 by 1944.[3] However, there was no major repopulation of skid row in the immediate postwar period. The expected depression never materialized, and the Veterans Administration combined with the G.I. Bill of Rights helped most soldiers return to a normal civilian life.

The skid row community has continued to decrease in size for most of the postwar period. The Bowery, which housed 75,000 in the 1919 recession, and 15,000 in 1949, had a population of only 5,400 in the mid-1960s.[4] Continued high aggregate demand, and improved welfare and pension benefits helped keep men off the row. Moreover, there was a decreasing supply of unskilled jobs available for the skid row resident. The mechanization of agriculture, lumbering, and construction, along with the decline of the railroads, vastly reduced the number of men employed in mobile occupations. Within the cities themselves, jobs like shoveling snow, washing dishes, and cleaning streets were largely replaced by machines. Not only automation, but also unionization and perhaps minimum wage laws reduced the number of casual employment possibilities for the disaffiliated and somewhat unreliable skid row man.

INHABITANTS

The composition of skid row has changed considerably since the Depression. Skid row no longer serves as an employment center[5] and has been abandoned by the young independent worker. Those remaining on the row are the worst cases, often the hard core of the unemployables. The typical resident is older, poorer, and more physically debilitated than his Depression counterpart. Skid row has become almost exclusively an open asylum for the derelict, and an old-age rest home for the very poor.

Skid row is inhabitated almost entirely by males. There are no children and virtually no women. In the 1960s, the median age of the skid row man was over fifty. Almost two-thirds had never married; some 20 percent were divorced. Seventy percent were physically handicapped to such an extent that it restricted their capacity to hold a normal job, though only one in ten was unable to work at all. Some 40 percent worked at least part time, as railway workers, farm laborers, seamen, dishwasters, or on other low-status, low-skill, poor-paying jobs. Some one-third were very heavy drinkers, one-third fairly heavy drinkers, while the rest drank little, if at all. The vast majority were Caucasians. In many cities, skid rows were white islands in predominantly minority areas.[6]

Most skid row men live in old cubicle hotels. The cubicles are always tiny, and the hotels often dirty, noisy, and filled with the stench of vomit. The illness and morbidity rate of skid row men is quite high. The tuberculosis death rate in Chicago's skid row is thirty-seven times higher than the normal rate for adult males; the heart-disease death rate is 233 times higher, and pneumonia fourteen times as high. On a typical winter day, about one-fourth of the men are incapacitated by illness.[7]

Skid row is not a pleasant place to live. Accommodations are atrocious, contagious disease is prevalent, and the outside world views residents with disdain and disgust. Not surprisingly, most inhabitants indicate that they are not very happy living on the row.[8]

ECONOMIC APPROACH

If skid row is so awful, why do men move there? In-migration is required, for virtually no one is born on the row. Sociologists and psychologists have a variety of possible answers: men live on the row because of personality disorganization, undersocialization, lack of social integration, refusal to assume responsibility, or alienation from society's basic cultural values.[9] The economic approach is somewhat different. The crucial assumption is that humans are rational, calculating, utility-maximizing beings, and skid-rowers are as normal in this respect as are suburbanites or rural dwellers, academicians, politicians, or criminals. Men move to skid row because it is, or seems to be, the best option they have. Skid row life seems better for them than any other available alternative. The public-policy implications of the economic approach are that if you want men to voluntarily leave skid row, changes must be made in the perceived costs and benefits of this versus other potential residence locations.

Studies do indicate that the basic reasons men move to skid row are economic, principally because it is a very cheap place to live, but also since secondary employment is potentially available, and private missions are located there to provide temporary assistance.[10] The fact that normal material incentives predominate in the skid row location decision does provide some support for the utility maximization hypothesis as a useful first step in understanding the skid row man.

The high visibility and alternate life-style offered by skid row has produced a great deal of sociological research, but has never attracted the attention of economists. Yet there seem to be many issues about which economists could contribute worthwhile insights. Labor economists should have interesting things to say about the migratory, temporary, and secondary aspects of skid row employment and the changing supply of jobs available to the skid row man. Development economists might view skid row as a colonial area and discuss the influence of trade, aid, foreign investment, and other actions taken by the advanced outside world. Macroeconomists could better study the impact of aggregate policies on skid row size and life. There are also issues to be addressed by public finance economists, as well as those interested in income distribution and private charity. This chapter takes something of the approach of an urban economist. It briefly discusses crime in skid row, and then the public policy issue of skid row dispersal.

CRIME

The law occupies a very central position in the life of the skid row man—the typical skid row resident averages three or four arrests per year! The charge is invariably public drunkenness, disorderly conduct, or vagrancy.[11] The policy of the police toward skid row is generally one of containment. Police officers are usually on permanent assignment to skid row. They are expected to preserve the peace, but are given wide discretionary authority to achieve this goal. This discretionary power of the skid row cop has made him a prime candidate for minor bribes.[12]

In 1960, arrests for public drunkenness alone accounted for 38 percent of all arrests made in the United States. Although only 3 percent of a city's alcoholics normally live on skid row, the row houses over 40 percent of those arrested for drunkenness.[13] While public drunkenness is more likely to be tolerated in skid row areas, which is one reason alcoholics live there, the absence of friends and relatives to protect and control the indigent, homeless man makes him a prime target for incarceration. Police may arrest the skid row man just to keep him from being rolled. They make more arrests in the winter to prevent drunks from passing out and freezing to death. Jail is seen as a clean, quiet place to sleep it off. Moreover, police realize that arrest creates little inconvenience for the skid-rower: work time may not be lost, for most are unemployed; broken commitments are few, for responsibility is rare; and friends and family are not upset, for there are no close relationships.

Skid row would seem to play a central role not only in aggregate U.S. crime statistics, but more important, in court time and expense. But skid row cases are handled expeditiously, if not always equitably. Drunk court tends to operate on an assembly-line basis, with trial times ranging from thirty seconds to four minutes.[14] In the long run, however, incarceration costs remain relatively high for the taxpayer (and the drunk) because jail serves merely as a place of confinement, rather than rehabilitation. Indigent alcoholics usually become trapped in a revolving-door cycle: intoxication, arrest, conviction, confinement, release, and subsequent reintoxication. A very generous evaluation of the current system of justice comes from the President's Commission on Law Enforcement and Administration of Justice:

> The criminal justice system appears ineffective to deter drunkenness or to meet the problems of the chronic alcoholic offender. What the system usually does accomplish is to remove the drunk from public view, detoxify him, and provide him with food, shelter, emergency medical service, and a period of forced sobriety. As presently constituted, the system is not in a position to meet his underlying medical and social problems.[15]

Incarceration does at least keep the drunk off the streets for a time period. This decreases panhandling and littering, and generally improves the neighborhood appearance. Before large conventions or celebrations there are usually a significant number of skid row arrests, designed to clean up the area.[16] But such arrests have little effect on the safety of the average citizenry, for chronic alcoholics rarely commit offenses against the person. Instead they, and indeed all skid row inhabitants, are the frequent victims of violent crimes.

Jackrollers find ready victims among skid row's elderly men and heavy drinkers. It is not difficult to force such a man into a darkened doorway or alley, to rob him, and, if desired, to administer a brutal kicking and beating in the process. Afterward, the victim may not remember or be able to recognize his assailant, or he may fear retaliation if he calls the police. At any rate, the courtroom testimony of a derelict does not carry much weight. Most important, the skid row man is an easy prey for criminals because, while often gregarious, he does not usually develop bonds of friendship or a sense of community. An unaffiliated man has no allies to turn to. One observer sees skid row social interaction as manifesting

> the norm of non-interference, a certain placid acceptance of things as they are. . . . The curious, callous indifference which surrounds acts of violence, assaults, robberies, and so on in the Bowery bars and on the Bowery streets is the product of a fundamental denial of the creation of casual responsibilities. The Bowery man is, first and foremost not his brother's keeper.[17]

Protecting his meager possessions can be a major problem for the skid row man. One-third of Philadelphia's skid row residents were jackrolled in 1959, and 13 percent had been robbed three or more times in that twelve-month period.[18] The fear of the jackroller increases the value of hotels that provide at least a modicum of security. And being robbed by drinking companions seems to make men wary of casual acquaintances, cynical about friendship, and less likely to establish lasting social bonds.

For some criminals, skid row is a good place to hide from the police. The appearance of a stranger in the area produces little comment and arouses few suspicions. Cubicle hotels require little identification. The high-density male population makes it easy to remain anonymous. But successful criminals rarely come to skid row; it is simply too disagreeable a place to live.

The skid row jackroller is generally a resident of the row. He is not a successful person, nor a successful criminal. While skid row does have an abundance of easy marks, the pickings per victim are very slim. Stealing an old man's pension check or his shoes does not yield large profits. Prosperous felons do not usually rob skid row men. There is little to gain, much to lose.

But normal criminal sanctions have little effect aginst the resident jackroller. His potential costs from arrest and imprisonment are small. He has no reputation to be ruined, no family to be humiliated, and no large income to be lost. Moreover, the likelihood of being caught and convicted is low. Thus, not only do petty thieves sometimes move to the row, but skid row men often turn into felons. It is not surprising that skid row areas are packed with the small-time, unsuccessful, but sometimes violent criminal.

DISPERSAL

Skid row is a special kind of slum, a clustering of low-income homeless men in a mixed commercial and residential area. It is created in a manner similar to other city slums. A skid row may be formed when an elevated railroad is built through an already declining retail/residential area. The noise, and the absence of sunlight, make property values fall precipitously. Higher-income families move out, and higher-income shoppers stay away. Low-income people are attracted to this area of falling rents, but declining amenities. Individual building owners may have little incentive to improve or repair their units in the face of declining neighborhood values. The area continues to decay, and becomes a slum.

An area becomes a skid row rather than a ghetto when homeless men abound in sufficient numbers to repel normal low-income households. Skid row is a horrible place to raise a family, much worse than the usual slum; most single women also feel they are better off elsewhere. Soon the tract of land becomes completely inhabited by the skid row man. Areas most suitable for skid row slums are those where dwellings are easily convertible into cheap cubicle hotels, and where the zoning laws permit saloons and inexpensive restaurants that cater to the homeless man. In the past, locations that became skid rows were also near jobs suitable for the cheap, part-time, somewhat unreliable, but highly mobile worker. Older skid rows are thus often situated in run-down areas adjacent to waterfronts, freight yards, trucking and storage depots.

In the postwar period, high aggregate demand combined with mechanization, unionzation, and improved welfare, pension and veterans' benefits have served to decrease the size of the skid row community. In addition, certain government policies in the 1960s were aimed directly at eliminating skid row areas. These policies included enforcement of tougher building codes and zoning laws, and most specifically, urban renewal. Urban renewal demolished old skid row areas in a large number of cities including Detroit, Minneapolis, St. Louis, Boston, Philadelphia, and San Francisco. Generally the row merely shifted locations. In San Francisco, for example, a new skid row emerged less than three blocks from the old one, while in Philadelphia, smaller skid rows appeared in a number of distinct locations.[19]

Urban renewal does not necessarily imply an explicit policy of slum resident dispersal, but it can often be a major first step in that direction. Much has been written about the pros and cons of urban renewal and ghetto dispersal. The attempt here is less to recapitulate the arguments than to highlight some of the crucial differences between dispersing skid row men and dispersing the inhabitants of black urban slums.

The dispersal of the black ghetto has been advocated for a number of reasons. Dispersal would allow blacks to reside closer to their employment and to learn more about suburban job opportunities. It should provide better housing alternatives for them. It could also increase racial integration and quality education. Skid row dispersal brings no such potential gains, for the skid row man is more likely to be unemployable. He lives in a community shrinking in population rather than one that is overflowing. And not only does he have no children, but he is typically a Caucasian in a larger black community. His dispersal might well tend to increase minority concentration in the center city.

Of course, dispersal of the skid row man may provide some social benefits. Central-city blight could decrease. Crime and addiction, which often breed in such concentrations, would probably diminish. Also, removing the skid row label and forcing increased interaction between the homeless man and normal society might improve his chances for reaffiliation.[20]

But the problems of dispersal can be large. There are the immediate and direct costs of forcing people to move. The skid row man, if a utility-maximizer, is made worse off, for he would otherwise have relocated himself. Moreover, dispersal seems not to diminish the number of disaffiliated men, but merely to disperse them.[21] And dispersal not only creates problems elsewhere, but probably increases overall public care and control costs. It seems easier to provide publicly for the homeless if they are geographically concentrated. The same is true for the containment of undesirable deviants.

CONCLUSION

Economists view the skid row man, even the alcoholic, as a rational utility maximizer. He moves to the row because, however squalid, this is the best place available for him to live. The clustering of disaffiliated men in skid row communities enables facilities to thrive—flophouses, saloons, missions—that specialize in servicing their needs. At one time skid row served as an employment center for the highly mobile, unskilled laborer. The dispersal of skid row men means the elimination of these positive external effects of agglomeration. Public dispersal policy thus seems to make sense only if the negative externalities, such as crime promotion, greatly outweigh the positive consequences of concentration.

The recent direct policy attempts at skid row elimination have been more instrumental in shifting skid rows than in reducing them. That skid rows have decreased in size is primarily due to the changed economic environment since the Depression. Presently there are indications that skid row is going through another major transformation. The cause is the breaking of racial barriers, with young blacks infiltrating the predominantly white row. The growing numbers of young people have caused an increase in violent crimes, forcing many of the aged indigent to leave the area. The overall effect has been a slight increase in total population, and a radical change in its composition. Skid row is becoming more and more the domain of the alcoholic, the drug addict, and the unemployed young black.[22] It is a far different place from the hobohemia of the thirties or the skid row of the sixties when urban renewal was in full bloom.

FOR DISCUSSION

1. Take a branch of economics and analyze skid row from that perspective. For instance, what questions would a radical economist ask about skid row?

2. According to an economist, why are men disaffiliated? What is the connection between income and disaffiliation?

3. What are the costs to society of public drunkenness? of vagrancy? of a skid row area?

4. What will be the effect on skid row of the Great Recession of the mid-1970s?

5. What are the principal effects of the most recent transformation of skid row?

6. What kinds of policies would prove most effective in eliminating skid row? What policies are optimal from the point of view of society?

NOTES TO CHAPTER SEVENTEEN

1. Samuel E. Wallace, *Skid Row as a Way of Life* (Totowa, N.J.: Bedminster Press, 1965), pp. 13-19.
2. Ibid., p. 18.
3. Ibid., p. 22.
4. Howard Bahr, "The Gradual Disappearance of Skid Row," *Social Problems* 15(Summer 1967):42.
5. David Levinson, "Skid Row in Transition," *Urban Anthropology* 3(1974):84.

6. Donald J. Bogue, *Skid Row in American Cities*, (Chicago: University of Chicago Press, 1963), pp. 92–390; Howard M. Bahr, *Skid Row: Introduction to Disaffiliation* (New York: Oxford University Press, 1973), pp. 87–148.

7. Bogue, *Skid Row in American Cities*, pp. 199–230.

8. Bahr, *Skid Row*, p. 164.

9. Wallace, *Skid Row as a Way of Life*, p. 130.

10. Bogue, *Skid Row in American Cities*, p. 308.

11. Ibid., p. 281.

12. Wallace, *Skid Row as a Way of Life*, p. 96; Bahr, *Skid Row;* pp. 231–33.

13. Bahr, pp. 227–28.

14. Wallace, p. 103.

15. President's Commission on Law Enforcement and Administration of Justice, *Task Force Report: Drunkenness*, (Washington, D.C.: U.S. Government Printing Office, 1967), p. 3.

16. Wallace, p. 103.

17. Theodore Caplow, transcript of Homeless Project staff meeting, Bureau of Applied Research, 25 February 1965, cited in Bahr, p. 163.

18. L.U. Blumberg, T.E. Shipley, J.O. Moor, "The Skid Row man," *Quarterly Journal of Studies on Alcohol* 32(December 1971):922.

19. Ibid., pp. 931–35.

20. Bahr, *Skid Row:* p. 285.

21. Bahr, "Gradual Disappearance of Skid Row," p. 44.

22. Levinson, "Skid Row in Transition," pp. 85–87; E. Rubington, "Changing Skid Row," *Quarterly Journal of Studies in Alcohol* 32(March 1971):130–132.

Chapter 18

The Bible

When I was young I was told that there was "baseball in the Bible." It commenced with "in the beginning" (in the big inning) and included Golaith being beaned, Abraham sacrificing, and Noah catching a couple of flies. There was an early prohibition against stealing, as well as people striking out, walking, and, of course, making errors. At the time I though all this was pretty clever. The present chapter must be considered in the same broad genre. It is a short, light treatment of "economics in the Bible."

This paper is not about religion, nor the effects of religion on eonomics or economic development. It is about a great and influential literary work, the Holy Bible, and tries to illuminate "how an economist might read the Good Book." The focus of the paper is on the most fundamental concept in economics, the notion of scarcity, especially with respect to the story of the creation and the teachings of Jesus.

It all started wtih Adam and Eve. In that Garden of Eden where grew "every tree that is pleasant to the sight, and good for food," there was no scarcity. Material goods were plentiful. Supplies exceeded desires, and life was sweet. There was no economic problem and no need for economists. This, indeed, was a paradise.

Then Eve ate the apple. Tempted, she succumbed. She was not following her long-run self-interest. She appears to have been a poor utility maximizer. It might be said that she was simply trying to become like a god; but this was a vain desire that could not be satisfied.

At any rate, if you dislike studying economics, put the blame where it belongs. The fault lies with Eve (and that serpent).

Some might argue that Eve simply hastened the inevitable. Following God's command to "be fruitful and multiply," man soon would have overpopulated Eden and eventually the earth. Perhaps the economic problem was just around the corner. We cannot say. But we do know that the eating of the apple so angered God that he cursed the ground, forcing man to live by the sweat of his brow. It may have been then that he made man mortal, "for dust thou art, and unto dust shalt thou return." Mortality firmly established that greatest of opportunity costs, time, for man's time on earth was scarce. And, of course, the knowledge of good and evil made Adam and Eve aware of their nakedness, creating a new demand, the need and desire for clothing.

Since the day that Adam and Eve were thrown out of Eden, man has known scarcity. In the teachings of Jesus we find a new attempt to ameliorate "the economic problem." Jesus' method was not to increase the supply of goods (though he did this on occasion), but to urge man to limit his material desires. The story of the rich young man who followed the ten commandments and yearned for eternal life is told repeatedly in the gospels. Jesus said to him: "If thou wilt be perfect, go and sell that thou hast, and give to the poor, and thou shall have treasure in heaven: and come and follow me." He continued: "It is easier for a camel to go through the eye of a needle, than for a rich man to enter the kingdom of God."

An economist perceives this argument in terms of tradeoffs, choices between this life and the next. Riches here will mean pain and unhappiness in the afterlife. It is the meek and the poor in spirit who will receive their "treasures" in heaven. Those who would follow Jesus and his ethical teachings will find their material needs are few. Would all society follow him, total material desires would be much less than potential production, the bliss point well inside the production-possibility frontier. People's material demands would be met, and, as Jesus argues, their spiritual needs as well.

For Jesus, the choice between this life and the next is easy. "The kingdom of heaven," he said, "is like unto a merchant man, seeking goodly pearls, who when he found one pearl of great price, went and sold all that he had and bought it." That pearl, the attainment of heaven, is to be valued above all else. It is the supreme goal of the wise man. One should make no tradeoffs. "For what shall it profit a man, if he shall gain the whole world, and lose his own soul? or what shall a man give in exchange for his soul?" For Jesus, the price of a soul is infinite. Remember, for those not gaining admittance to the kingdom of heaven, there shall be a "wailing and gnashing of teeth."

Jesus seems to have seen man as too unenlightened to perceive the tradeoff between riches in this life, and heaven in the next, and/or too tempted by the immediate pleasures of worldly wealth. His preachings were designed to correct this situation, to reiterate the teachings of the prophets. "Lay not up for yourselves treasures upon earth," he urges, "but lay up for yourselves treasures in heaven." And continuing, "No man can serve two masters. . . . Ye cannot serve God and Mammon." Or as Paul writes to Timothy: "The love of money is the root of all evil." Not surprisingly, this fundamental biblical argument is not usually heeded by modern Christians. Perhaps if it were, there would again be little need for economics or economists.

In all his teachings, Jesus' basic conception of man seems quite similar to the economist's. Man tries to follow his own self-interest, weighing the costs and benefits of various alternatives. Therefore, the way to change man's behavior is to change the payoffs for particular courses of action, or at least change man's perception of the payoffs. This latter seems Jesus' principal role on earth.

For example, Jesus favored giving to the poor and needy. Thus, his arguments to sway men appeal not to their virtue or their social responsibility, but directly to their rational self-interest. "When thou makest a dinner, or a supper," he said, "call not thy friends, nor thy brethren, neither thy kinsmen, nor thy rich neighbors; lest they also bid thee again, and a recompense be made thee. But when thou makest a feast, call the poor, the maimed, the lame, the blind: And thou shalt be blessed, for they cannot recompense thee: for thou shalt be recompensed at the resurrection of the just." In other words, give to the poor, for then you will be blessed by God. Such good deeds will be rewarded in the afterlife, just as wicked ones will be punished.

Jesus not only gave spiritual comfort to the poor, but also healed diseases and cast out devils. Because the price he charged for these services was so low, queuing resulted, and a competition for favors. The multitudes attracted to him had, at times, to be fed, and this Jesus accomplished by miraculously increasing the supply of bread and fishes; he is also known to have converted water into wine. In our more enlightened era, this practice of freely distributing such scarce material goods could be construed as "dumping" and would certainly be regarded unkindly by the bread, wine, and fishing industries.

In his own day, Jesus did incur great disfavor with the vested interests. He attacked the religious and ruling elite: "Woe unto you, scribes and Pharisees, hypocrites!" And his actions, such as casting out "all them that sold and bought in the temple" and overthrowing the tables of the money-changers, seemed disruptive of banking and exchange and indeed of the entire economic as well as social fabric of the community. He was killed forthwith.

CONCLUSION

Economists have a particular way of looking at the world. They make certain assumptions, and focus on certain aspects of society. The economic approach can be applied to a variety of social phenomena. This paper was a brief, light account of the way some biblical stories struck one economist.

> Of making many books there is no end;
> And much study is a weariness of the flesh.
> (Ecclesiastes)

FOR DISCUSSION

1. What is the effect of burnt (or unburnt) sacrifices on gross national product? On economic welfare? On social well-being?

2. "A virtuous woman who can find/For her price is far above rubies." Can the price of a virtuous woman be put in monetary terms? Should it be? Could putting an economic value on things or relationships in any way "cheapen" them?

3. "A Christian is simply an economic man with special beliefs." Comment.

4. How might an economist view the ten commandments? For example:

"Remember the Sabbath, to keep it holy." Does this imply blue laws and forced leisure?

"Thou shalt not covet." What are the implications for consumer interdependence?

"Thou shalt not steal." What are the implications about the type of economic system? about the cost of law enforcement?

"Thou shalt have no other gods before me." Is there any relationship between monotheism/pantheism and monopoly/competition?

5. How important, do you think are religious beliefs in affecting economic development? How important are religious institutions? How does the economic system affect religious beliefs and institutions.

✳ *Appendix*

Payoff Matrices

A payoff matrix provides a useful tool for describing and analyzing a wide variety of situations, interactions, and "games." Here we briefly examine a very simple kind of situation; there are two players, and each has two options. There are thus four possible outcomes.

Consider a pure conflict situation. You and your friend are "bucking up," or flipping for nickels. If you match, you win; if you don't, he wins. In figure A–1 you are row and he is column. His payoffs are given in parentheses. This pure conflict situation is called a zero-sum game. Whatever you win, he loses, and vice versa. Note that the payoffs in each possible outcome sum to zero. In this simple game it can never improve your situation to go first, or to let your opponent know your selection ahead of time. You should be able to draw the payoffs if two people play "rock, paper and scissors" for quarters. Games such as poker, chess, and monopoly may be considered more complicated zero-sum games.

At the other extreme of pure conflict games are pure coordination games. These are cooperative rather than competitive situations. TV's "Match Game," where contestants and celebrities try to give identical answers, is a successful game show based on pure coordination.

Consider this real-world example. You are supposed to meet your friend Fred at the outdoor tennis courts at 5:00. At 4:40 it begins to mist. You are not sure whether it will clear up or rain and eliminate the possibility of tennis. You cannot locate Fred, nor can he reach you. You thus have two possible choices: to go (walk) to the courts, or not to. Fred has similar options. There are thus four possible out-

187

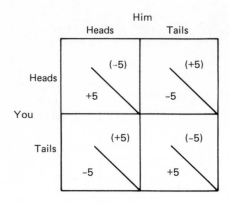

Figure A-1.

comes. From your perspective, it is important that you both make the same choice. If you both go, that is fine: if the sun shines, you can play tennis, and if it rains you can go together for a beer. If neither of you goes, that is also fine, for you have other things you can be doing. But if one of you goes, while the other doesn't, that is not so good. You will be unhappy if you go, and wait, and he never shows up. You will also be unhappy if Fred goes, and waits, and becomes annoyed at you. Your payoffs (in utils) are given in figure A-2. If Fred has identical preferences, the game is one of pure coordination (figure A-3).

You would definitely like to be able to inform Fred of your choice. Even if you couldn't communicate directly, it would be very helpful to have a signal to help you coordinate. Perhaps you might have agreed beforehand to telephone WEATHER in such a contin-

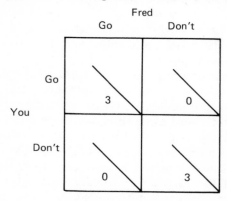

Figure A-2.

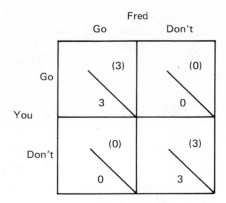

Figure A-3.

gency, and if the chance of rain were less than 70 percent you both would go. Or you could call a mutual friend, tell him your decision, and have him relay the message. Or better still, you could have pre-arranged a time and number for one to call the other, and agreed on your decision if no call were made.

Let us change the game a bit by postulating that Fred enjoys his walk to the tennis court—even in the rain. He prefers to meet you, but in any event, he enjoys his "constitutional." And you know this. The payoffs in this new "game" are given below. We assume that any form of communication is impossible, and no prearrangements have been made. Should you go or not?

An easier question is: Should Fred go or not? As in most economic models, we assume that individuals are, or try to be, rational utility

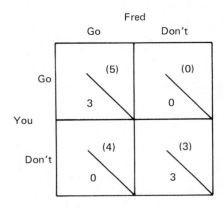

Figure A-4.

maximizers. And any (dis)utility that Fred receives from your happiness or misery is already included in his payoffs. Making these assumptions, we can say that Fred should go. Fred has a "dominant strategy." No matter what you do, he is better off going. Assume he knows you will go; then he too should go, and receive 5 rather than 0 utils. Assume he knows you aren't going; then he should still go, and receive 4 rather than 3 utils. Your choice doesn't affect his decision. He cares about your choice, however, because it does affect his payoffs.

If Fred has a dominant strategy, and you know it and believe him rational, then you will expect him to follow his dominant strategy. You will expect him to go. And if he goes, then so should you, and receive 3 rather than 0 utils. In this particular game, if both parties act rationally, no communication is needed to reach the optimal solution for both.

Sometimes decision-makers following their own self-interest reach an inferior outcome. This is best illustrated by the "prisoner's dilemma" game. Consider this scenerio. Two men meet in a bar; they are complete strangers. They decide to commit a burglary, and do so successfully. They divide the loot and expect never to see each other again. Unfortunately for them, they are both apprehended and taken before the district attorney. The D.A. knows about game theory, and devises an ingenious scheme. Before the criminals can communicate with each other, he separates them, and tells each of them their options and (true) payoffs.

Within the next hour, each will have two choices: to confess or not to. There will thus be four possible outcomes for the criminals, as shown in figure A–5. If each confesses, each will receive a five-year sentence. If prisoner A confesses, while B does not, A will be allowed to turn state's evidence, and get off scot free. B will be prosecuted to the full extent of the law, and will receive ten years in jail. The reverse is true if B confesses while A does not. If neither confesses, the D.A. has enough evidence to put them both away for two years. The payoff matrix is given below. What should the prisoners do?

Each has a dominant strategy, and that is to confess. For example, no matter what B does, A is better off confessing. Suppose A hears B tell his lawyer that he (B) is going to confess. Then A should also confess, since by doing so he will receive five rather than ten years. Suppose, on the other hand, A learns that B is going to keep silent. A should still confess. By confessing, he is not forced to go to jail; if he refuses to confess, he gets two years. Since the game is perfectly symmetrical, B has an identical dominant strategy.

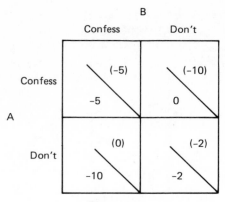

Figure A-5.

In a prisoner's dilemma game, participants have a dominant strategy. But if each follows that dominant strategy, if each follows his own self-interest, they will arrive at a domin*ated* outcome. In other words, they could *both* be better off if they acted differently. Criminals A and B would both prefer that both refuse to confess. Then each would receive only two years in jail, rather than five. Unfortunately for them, without some form of binding contract, each has a strong incentive to confess.

Interestingly, they are more likely to reach the preferred outcome (from their perspective) if certain payoffs are made *worse*. Assume that although they are strangers, both belong to the same organization, such as the Mafia, that provides severe penalties (loss of eyes, tongue, fingers) for anyone who confesses. If this threat is credible, the prisoners may be facing a situation such as described in figure A-6. Now each has a dominant strategy *not* to confess. If each follows his own self-interest, neither will confess, and they will serve only 2 years.

Payoff matrices can usefully be applied to a wide range of situatins involving decisions. For example, in interpersonal relations, should you send Christmas cards to particular friends? How should others be addressed in speech? What type of clothes should be worn to a certain function? What time should you arrive at the party? In international relations, payoff matrices might be useful in analyzing whether Country A should recognize Country B. Should it attack Country B? Should battling countries use germ warfare? Should prisoners be exchanged? Should nuclear bombs be employed? And so forth. Payoff matrices are often helpful in highlighting the crucial aspects of the game: how many parties are participating, how many

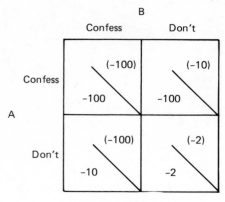

Figure A-6.

times the game will be played, whether the parties meet in other games, what information is available, whether communication is possible, and what tactics and strategies can prove effective.

The best way for the reader to begin to understand payoff matrices is to draw them, and play simple simulated games.

SOURCES

R. Duncan Luce and Howard Raiffa, *Games and Decisions* (New York: John Wiley and Sons, Inc., 1957).

Thomas C. Schelling, *The Strategy of Conflict* (New York: Oxford University Press, Galaxy, 1963).

Index